A LITURGIST'S GUIDE TO INCLUSIVE LANGUAGE

Ronald D. Witherup, S.S.

A Liturgical Press Book

 THE LITURGICAL PRESS
Collegeville, Minnesota

Nihil obstat: Robert C. Harren, J.C.L., *Censor deputatus.*
Imprimatur: ✛ John F. Kinney, Bishop of St. Cloud, January 15, 1996.

Cover design by Greg Becker

1	2	3	4	5	6	7	8

Library of Congress Cataloging-in-Publication Data

Witherup, Ronald D., 1950–
    A liturgist's guide to inclusive language / Ronald D. Witherup.
        p.   cm.
    Includes bibliographical references.
    ISBN 0-8146-2257-7
    1. Sexism in liturgical language.   2. Catholic Church—United States—Liturgy.   I. Title.
    BX1970.W57   1996
    264′.02′0014—dc 20   95-16423
                                                                              CIP

A LITURGIST'S GUIDE
TO INCLUSIVE LANGUAGE

For Dorothy

Contents

Table of Abbreviations ix

Preface xi

Introduction 1

I. Analysis of the Context 7
   A. Social Context 7
      1. Importance of Language 8
      2. Describing Exclusive and Inclusive
         Language 9
      3. Terminological Differences 11
      4. Bishops' Guidelines and the Social
         Context 12

   B. Theological Context 13
      1. The Mystery of God 14
      2. Biblical Testimony 14
      3. Liturgical Underpinnings of the
         Church 15

   C. Local Context 17

II. The Principles of Inclusive Language 19

   A. Three General Principles 19

   B. Applied Principles.........................21
      1. References to People, Persons 21
      Texts That Denigrate the Status
      of Women 25

2. References to God 27
    a. The Nature of God-Talk 28
    b. Patriarchal Language in Titles 30
    c. Feminine Imagery for God 33
    d. The Trinity 36
       God the Father 37
       Abba 38
       God the Son 41
       God the Spirit 46

III. Practical Guidelines for Inclusive Language
     in Liturgy 49

IV. Ongoing Developments 56

    A. Brief History of the Controversy 56

    B. Disputed Issues 58
       1. Designations for Human Beings 59
       2. Christological Concerns 60

    C. A Pastoral Example 63
    D. Remaining Questions 65

V. The Challenge of the Future 67

    A. Summary Statements 67

    B. Call to Conversion 70

Glossary 75

Appendix: The American Bishops' Guidelines 77

Selected Annotated Bibliography for
Further Reading 87

Index to Scripture Citations 96

Table of Abbreviations

AAR/SBL	American Academy of Religion/Society of Biblical Literature
AAS	*Acta Apostolicae Sedis* (Rome, 1909–)
BR	*Bible Review*
BTB	*Biblical Theology Bulletin*
BToday	*The Bible Today*
CCCB	Canadian Conference of Catholic Bishops
CBQ	*The Catholic Biblical Quarterly*
HTR	*Harvard Theological Review*
JB	*The Jerusalem Bible* (Doubleday, 1966)
JBL	*Journal of Biblical Literature*
JTS	*Journal of Theological Studies*
NABRNT	*The New American Bible with Revised New Testament* (Confraternity of Christian Doctrine, 1986)
NCR	*The National Catholic Reporter*
NEB	*The New English Bible* (Oxford, 1976)
NJB	*The New Jerusalem Bible* (Doubleday, 1985)
NRSV	*New Revised Standard Version* (Oxford, 1989)
PerRS	*Perspectives in Religious Studies*
Psalms	*The Revised Psalms of the New American Bible* (Catholic Book Publishing, 1991)
REB	*The Revised English Bible* (Oxford, 1989)
SJT	*Scottish Journal of Theology*
TToday	*Theology Today*
TS	*Theological Studies*

USCC   United States Catholic Conference
USQR   *Union Seminary Quarterly Review*

Preface

This book has been gestating for some twelve years. It grew out of various experiences in ministry in the context of Roman Catholic seminaries and parishes and in conversation with many priests, religious, and lay people who are concerned about the issue of inclusive language. My first contact with the notion that there was even a problem was in the late 1970s while, as a young priest, I was in a year-long sabbatical program in California. The frustration, hurt, and anger that many women in the program, both lay and religious, experienced was palpable and a moving eye opener for me. Some of the emotion stemmed from insensitive mistreatment by Church leaders, especially pastors and other priests, but some of it seemed to originate from less tangible experiences that summed up what being a woman in a male dominated social and ecclesial environment meant. I learned a lot in the course of the year. I found my own attitudes changing (slowly, to be sure) and my ability to comprehend the interior depth of emotional suffering experienced by women in many situations growing.

I myself have reached a point where I, along with many men and women, cringe at needlessly exclusive language. But my own experience has been somewhat double-edged. If I have learned to be empathetic with women who feel powerless in a patriarchally dominated society, nevertheless I have also felt my own discomfort with what at times struck me as a reverse oppression. In some situations with women, while I could not disguise the fact that I was a male, admitting that I was a priest as well was tantamount to confessing participation in some vile male conspiracy to subjugate women. I became determined to seek out an acceptable path through this dual experience. Even some feminists would admit that we will begin to liberate women when we also liberate men from the constraints of stereotypical behavior. In many situations in which I have found myself in ministry, such as a seminary Scripture professor and (earlier in my career) a director of liturgy, involvement with religious education conventions, parish adult enrichment sessions, retreats, and clergy education conferences, I have found that the issue of inclusive language is increasingly a prominent concern. Sometimes it simmers like a smoldering ember. At other times it bursts into a raging fire. Many women (and some men) sit through parish liturgies Sunday after Sunday and fume at what they experience as oppressive, exclusive, misogynistic language. Others actively set out to eradicate any perceived offensive language, sometimes with destructive and divisive results. Unfortunately, although informed people often have strong opinions one way or another about the issue, some others are either unscathed by the concern (perhaps totally insensitive and uninformed) or hostile to it (perhaps fearful and so defensive).

Inclusive language used to be viewed as a restricted concern of those in academia, far removed from the daily lives of ordinary people. But with rapid changes in society and with increased awareness of the issues involved, that situation is no longer the case. Many parishioners even in small, rural parishes will have at least heard about the notion of inclusive language, even though they may not have strong feelings one way or another. The recent controversy over the inclusive language of one major biblical translation (the *NRSV*), which erupted in late 1994 and which is recounted in chapter four, only points out further how far reaching are the concerns of this topic. My experience has indicated that helpful, practical resources are lacking on the rationale and technicalities of inclusive language that can be utilized on a parish level. This book attempts to fill the void.

As such, the goal of the book is threefold. First, it intends to inform and educate the average Catholic about some of the complexities of inclusive language. In this sense it is an exercise in consciousness raising. Second, it aims to provide a type of "handbook" for diocesan and parish liturgy groups, and for all liturgical ministers, who are often the ones who must respond to people's concerns in the local situation. In the absence of definitive directives in this delicate area, this book can offer at least some guidance to those who are concerned about language in liturgy. Third, it provides a resource for further study. The footnotes and a brief annotated bibliography for further reading are included to provide references of both theoretical and practical materials for those wishing to pursue the matter on their own.

I have also included a glossary of technical terms and an appendix containing the text of the American bishops' helpful guidelines on inclusive language. Given the often controverted nature of this issue, these guidelines provide a sensible and competent roadmap to negotiate the twists and turns that are inevitably encountered. They are the result of many years of consultation and research. They also reflect the views of the vast majority of American bishops (an eighty-one percent approval vote in 1990). The importance of the guidelines extends beyond usefulness for the scholars and bishops for whom they were intended. Their inclusion here as an appendix makes them available for study by a wider public.

Many people over the years have contributed to this study in one way or another. This book is an adaptation of guidelines for inclusive language originally developed in the context of consultation with liturgy committees in two Roman Catholic seminaries. I am grateful to colleagues and students at Theological College, Washington, D.C., St. Patrick's Seminary, Menlo Park, California, and St. Michael's College, Colchester, Vermont, to colleagues from the Catholic Biblical Association, and to many friends over the years, for their contributions to my own thoughts on the subject. I am especially grateful to Dr. Cecil White, librarian at St. Patrick's Seminary, who has helped me obtain research materials for this and other projects, and to my administrative assistant, Dr. Dorothy Tully. Naturally, I bear full responsibility for the shortcomings of this modest effort.[1]

---

1. The Roman Catholic orientation of this book is for pragmatic reasons only and does not preclude its usefulness in various ecumenical settings.

Introduction

Recent years have seen the problem of "exclusive" language in English grow in prominence as a point of theological debate.[2] This concern has had a practical impact on Roman Catholic liturgical celebrations throughout the United States. On a recent visit to a parish to preside at the Sunday celebration of the Eucharist, I was astonished to discover that a concerned and enthusiastic liturgy committee had paged through the entire Lectionary, expurgating every perceived example of exclusive language and writing in over the text their alternative rendering. The results were mixed; at times appropriate, at times barbaric, and in many instances a distortion of the underlying biblical text (in the original Hebrew or Greek).

While the question of inclusive language was recently studied by a committee of the National Conference of Catholic Bishops (NCCB),[3] careful guidelines for inclusive language have quite ob-

2. The magazine *Worship* has served as one vehicle for publishing articles on various aspects of this multifaceted topic. See the various listings in the annotated bibliography. They provide a rich resource of both theological analysis and bibliographical references for further reading.

3. See "Inclusive Language in Liturgy: Scriptural Texts," *Origins* 20 (November 29, 1990) 405–408, reprinted in the appendix of this book. References to this document used throughout this book will be given by paragraph number. Another committee of the NCCB was working on a pastoral letter addressing the concerns of women, though general consideration by the entire NCCB of this controversial document has been officially postponed.

viously not sifted down to the level of many parishes where decisions are being made about liturgical language, rubrics notwithstanding. In fact, the purpose of the Bishops' Guidelines was not to guide parish liturgists on *liturgical* matters, but to provide professional biblical translators and preparers of Lectionary and Sacramentary revisions appropriate guidelines on *biblical* translations.[4] But I believe something must be communicated about biblical and liturgical language to people on the parochial level, especially to those working with liturgy. My concern is that well-intentioned but misguided attempts on the local level to address the contemporary problem of exclusive/inclusive language may seriously miscommunicate the Word of God.

What can be done about liturgical language in light of this situation? Are we caught between some liturgical Scylla and Charybdis in which we perish by either being too cautious or too bold? To put it plainly, must we await further decisions from Church authorities before any action can be taken to correct a perpetually exclusive environment in liturgy? Or must we endure haphazard changes dictated by uninformed vigilante committees bent on correcting every perceived example of exclusive language regardless of context or background? Perhaps there is a middle course.

At the outset I must admit some trepidation about addressing this sensitive area. Inclusive language is an issue which rouses much tension and anxiety, especially in the Roman Catholic Church. Perhaps in line with other ecclesiastical realities, the tension surrounding this particular issue arises from two distinct approaches to the question.

On the one hand, some people (not only women, but many men as well) are so outraged by what they experience as the extreme exclusivity of Roman Catholic liturgy that they take it upon themselves to change (drastically at times) whatever they designate as offensive. They associate language with continued patriarchal oppression, symbolic of aeons of oppression of women and minorities in all kinds of situations throughout history. On the

---

4. For those unfamiliar with liturgical language, the Lectionary is the book of biblical readings used at Mass. It is divided into a three-year Sunday cycle and a two-year daily cycle of readings. The Sacramentary is the book of prayers and rubrics that the priest uses at the altar.

other hand, some people (including many in authoritative positions in the Church) feel that any discussion of inclusive language issues inevitably leads to a discussion of such controversial topics as the ordination of women. Some even view any consideration of this issue as yielding to the "sin" of feminism, in which women are inappropriately seeking privileges to which they have no right. Neither position reflects an adequate appraisal of the situation. But finding a middle path between two tenaciously held positions is no easy task. I am fully aware of the risk involved in taking the middle course. The enterprise may run aground on both fronts. Those who stridently want a complete and radical overhaul of liturgical language *now* may come away unsatisfied with the modest suggestions made in this book, feeling it is too timid to make a difference. The goal of some extremists is indeed to do away with the entire patriarchal system, not simply to reform language. Those who see the issue of inclusive language as a diabolical plot by feminists to destroy the Church will perhaps be aghast at the very thought of any change in the status quo. But I am convinced that the risk is worth taking in order that parish liturgical ministers may grasp at least some of the complexity of the issues involved and the urgency not to ignore but to address them.

In light of this emotionally charged situation, a few caveats are in order. First, this book will only address the narrow issue of inclusive language. No connection whatsoever is intended with other highly complex issues such as feminism in general or the ordination of women. Despite the tendency in some popular magazines automatically to connect the issue of inclusive language with the ordination of women, I do not accept that the two are intrinsically bound together.[5] Neither is this book a treatise on feminism as such or an attempt to address the question of reshaping a patriarchal society or Church. We will restrict our focus to biblical and liturgical language as it impacts on Catholic worship.

---

5. Pope John Paul II made the same connection in a brief address about "radical feminist" tendencies to some American bishops who were in Rome for their quinquennial ad limina visit, the visit required of bishops every five years to report to the Pope the status of their dioceses. See "On Parishes, Lay Ministry and Women," *Origins* 23:8 (July 15, 1993) 124–126.

Second, the limitations of my own perspective must be kept in mind. I write from the viewpoint of a seminary professor of Sacred Scripture to offer input from a biblical perspective on the question of inclusive language. I write as one passionately concerned about the treatment the Scriptures sometimes naively receive from uninformed positions and equally concerned about the emotional impact of language issues upon the women I have known and with whom I have worked over the years.

Third, although much of the literature that addresses the issue of inclusive language has been written by Protestants for their own liturgical situation, little has been written from a Roman Catholic perspective. We Catholics (thankfully, in my opinion, though extremists disagree) have a hierarchically organized Church. This structure inevitably entails certain restrictions and institutional constraints that other churches may not experience to the same degree. Nonetheless, I believe that Roman Catholics can and must address this issue forthrightly, for it is not just a passing fad. Inclusive language is a serious issue that affects our entire society, the Church included. Pope John Paul II recently phrased this concern well in an address to some American bishops: "Respect for women's rights is without doubt an essential step toward a more just and mature society, and the church cannot fail to make her own this worthy objective."[6] This statement occurs in the context of warning against the dangers of "radical feminism," which seeks to restructure the Church entirely, but it clearly insists that the Church cannot ignore the issue of women's rights in *both* society and Church.

Fourth, since a primary goal of this book is to give parish liturgists an orientation to the implications of inclusive language issues and to provide a guidebook for further research, readers are invited to enter the discussion on their own. One often hears complaints in parishes that much of current theological discussion does not quickly disseminate to the parish level. I hope that this book can at least give some educational direction on a parish level to this one particular biblical, liturgical, and theological issue.

Finally, the limited goal of this small book is unabashedly pragmatic. While it makes no pretense to address, let alone resolve,

---

6. Ibid., 126. See also his "Letters to Women," *Origins* 25:9 (July 27, 1995) 137–43.

all the issues about inclusive language, the book is based on the premise that we do not have to surrender to total inaction just because the issues are not immediately resolvable or because we await definitive action from Church leadership, which may take years to formulate. In fact, history indicates that changes in the Church often emerge from the local level. Not every change in the Church has come from the hierarchical structures of the Church. A recent example of such change in liturgy might be the alteration in the institution narrative of the Eucharistic Prayer. Long before the rubrics permitted the celebrant to refer to Christ shedding his blood for "all" rather than "all *men*," many priests had made the simple deletion of the offensive word. Of course, one cannot condone the violation of liturgical rubrics. I am merely pointing out that sometimes changes in the Church occur in this manner. Indeed this reality is somewhat analogous to the ancient principle of *lex orandi, lex credendi*. This Latin expression refers to the fact that the prayer life of the Church on a practical level has often influenced the development of doctrines that were defined at a later time. In this fashion the faith of the Church is always in relationship with the manner in which people pray.

In this regard, then, the contents of this book may be viewed as an *interim set of guidelines* that should prove useful in Roman Catholic parochial settings. These guidelines constitute a type of "handbook" to be used until such time as more definitive directives or solutions are forthcoming. As such, it strives simultaneously to respect both the current liturgical norms of the Church and the biblical texts used in the liturgy.

With these cautions in mind, we can proceed. The handbook consists of five chapters. The first chapter addresses the various contexts in which inclusive language issues arise. The second chapter sets forth general and applied principles for inclusive language regarding biblical texts. Chapter three outlines some practical guidelines for inclusive language in liturgy. The fourth chapter describes the recent Vatican controversy over inclusive language and discusses specific controversial texts. The final chapter summarizes major points and offers some thoughts about the challenge of the future.

Chapter I.

Analysis of the Context

The issue of inclusive language arises from at least three different but interrelated contexts. These are the social context that reflects society's concerns, the theological context that reflects the Church's concerns, and the local context of each individual congregation. We will examine each of these briefly to see how they impact upon the topic of inclusive language.

A. SOCIAL CONTEXT

Issues about inclusive language and, more broadly, the role of women in society are not just the concerns of a small minority. The implications of this turmoil in the Christian churches are seen to be far-reaching enough for society as to attract the frequent attention of the media. One popular news magazine even plastered its front cover with the title, "God and Women: A Second Reformation Sweeps Christianity."[7] This article was written in response to the Anglican Church's decision to admit women to the priesthood, but considerable attention was given to "masculine theol-

7. See the cover story in *Time* (November 23, 1992) 53–58. See also *Time* (October 26, 1992) 72, which has an article on inclusive language issues that were subsequently debated by the NCCB at its semiannual meeting in November 1992.

7

ogy" and issues of language. A national newspaper recently published an article entitled, "The Word Police Are Listening for 'Incorrect' Language," which largely focused on the issue of inclusivity.[8] It even pointed out that dictionaries are beginning to include appendices on "avoiding sexist language." In short, the issue is a prominent one in contemporary society, and it goes beyond the concern for mere "political correctness."

Another aspect of the social context is in the area of education. Virtually all public educational programs are sensitive to the need for inclusivity to some degree. Newer textbooks reflect this attitude, teachers are more aware of the issues, and children inevitably are being exposed to inclusivity issues in language and action. How ironic it would be if the only societal institution unfazed by such concerns to promote true equality and human dignity would be the Church!

1. Importance of Language

Many times I have heard women and men who oppose the use of inclusive language in the Church say, "What difference does it make? When I hear the word 'man' in the generic sense I understand that it includes all human beings, men and women together. Why do we need to change it?" Certainly in past eras, English words like "man" and "mankind" did have a generic meaning and were inclusive of all people regardless of gender. But language is a living, dynamic force in human existence. The way we say things, shaped by the words and expressions we use, does make a difference. Language not only reflects attitudes, but it also helps to *create* the reality around us. In fact, my hunch is that one factor in the resistance that many give to inclusive language is an unconscious fear that changing the language will indeed lead to real changes in the structure of daily life. For this reason many view inclusive language as a crucial issue that cannot be ignored.

If anyone doubts the importance of language, they only need to recall the ways in which miscommunication can so easily happen on a daily basis, for instance, in marriages. In her best-selling book, *You Just Don't Understand: Women and Men in Conversation,* Deborah Tannen analyzes innumerable examples of the ways

8. *The New York Times* (February 1, 1993) B1, 4.

in which men and women miscommunicate by language that reveals inner attitudes.[9] In the post-Freudian era, we have gotten used to the notion that "body language" reveals inner attitudes, but have we taken seriously how our words themselves can be revealing? Tannen's book shows that women and men do not think in the same way and thus do not express themselves in the same way. This divergence is often at the heart of marital discord. Her book is not about exclusive and inclusive language as such but points out that language really does matter in effective communication because it reflects thought and action. If women are increasingly experiencing some language as offensive, oppressive, or exclusive, and if that language reflects a deeply ingrained societal bias, then something must be done to address the situation, for language is only as effective as it communicates rather than miscommunicates.

2. Describing Exclusive and Inclusive Language

So far I have been using terms like exclusive and inclusive language as if they are self-evident. They are not. For the sake of clarity, I want to describe these terms more carefully as they are currently understood in the contemporary social context.

By *exclusive language,* I refer to any words or series of words whose meaning may be interpreted as pointing to one group or type of people and excluding others. The terms "exclusive/inclusive" are most often used to refer to language whose connotation is sexual or gender oriented. Exclusive language more broadly may also refer to words or expressions that have connotations of ethnicity, age, or physical characteristics. A few specific examples will be instructional.

One example is the expression "black and white," which often refers to a sharp dichotomy between two realities. This expression is now often perceived by people of color to be exclusive because it reflects a world view in which "white" is good and "black" is evil. Given the instances in American society and abroad of ongoing racism, language that perpetuates this dichotomy is certainly not helpful in building up racial tolerance and equality.

9. (New York: William Morrow, 1990). See also Wren, *Language,* 63–83.

Another example is the description of persons with physical, mental, or emotional handicaps. Rather than viewing them in totality as "the handicapped," sensitivity to inclusive language requires describing such people as "persons" with a particular disability. Thus a leper is more appropriately designated a *person* afflicted with leprosy (or Hansen's disease), or one who is deaf is a *person* whose hearing is impaired. Such an expression is seen as reinforcing first the dignity of the person, and only secondarily focusing on the particular disability. This principle of inclusivity is also a guideline used by the committee that is preparing a revision of the Roman Catholic Lectionary.

Yet a third example would be the expression "the Jews" used throughout John's Gospel to designate the opponents of Jesus. Despite appearances, it refers not to *all* Jews but to certain Jewish leaders at the time of Jesus, though it also reflects the hostility between Jews and Christians that developed at the time John's Gospel was written. A proper translation, especially for use in public proclamation of the Word of God, will try to take this factor into account.[10] The guidelines for those revising the Lectionary suggest alternatives such as "the Jewish authorities" or "the Jewish leaders" in keeping with the Church's previous guidelines on sensitivity to Jewish relations.[11]

Despite these broader issues of exclusive language, the primary focus for our purposes will be that which reflects *sexism*. In its broadest sense sexism is "belief that persons are superior or inferior to one another on the basis of their sex."[12] Sometimes the phrase "the language of patriarchy" is used to describe sexist language, an expression that emphasizes the dominance of male

10. Finding a good solution to this thorny translation problem is not easy. Gerard Sloyan's suggestion in his Interpretation Commentary on John (*John* [Atlanta: John Knox, 1988] xiii–xiv) that the term simply be left in its Greek form *hoi Ioudaioi* is certainly not practical. Would any congregation really understand such a term, even if it were used regularly? For an overview of this specific topic as it relates to preaching, see Ronald D. Witherup, "Preaching the Passion with Sensitivity to Judaism," *The Priest* 49:4 (1993) 12–16.

11. See *God's Mercy Endures Forever: Guidelines on the Presentations of Jews and Judaism in Catholic Preaching* (Washington, D.C.: USCC, 1988), and *Criteria for the Evaluation of Dramatizations of the Passion* (Washington, D.C.: USCC, 1988).

12. Margaret Farley, "Sexism," *New Catholic Encyclopedia*, 17:604.

lineage and hierarchically ordered structures. When referring to gender, "androcentrism" (from the Greek *anēr, andros* = "man") has gained currency. It is sometimes used as an umbrella term for sexism. Androcentrism describes the phenomenon of making characteristics of men *the* normative system in society. This stance not only underplays the role of women but, by word and action, discriminates against them. Sexist language, in particular, has become the most serious instance of exclusive language since it is expressive of centuries of misogyny and ill-treatment of women who constitute half the human race. Such exclusive language is evident in many levels of American society and has necessarily affected the liturgical life of the Church. Owing to the cultural influences of thousands of years, this use of language is reflected in the Bible, worship, and the very thought patterns of the Church.

In the positive sense, *inclusive language* as it applies to liturgy is that language that engages all people in the action of prayer and worship. It excludes no one; rather, all are invited equally into the liturgical experience. Such language fosters unity rather than division, a sense of belonging rather than displacement. Excising all exclusive language from the Bible or the regulated liturgical texts of the Church is not always possible, especially in the current situation of diverse responses to the entire issue of exclusive and inclusive language. But every worshiping community should acknowledge its own historical heritage (including exclusivity) and, at the same time, be committed to fostering inclusive language wherever possible.

3. Terminological Differences

A caution is in order concerning the terminology used in this handbook when discussing issues of inclusivity/exclusivity. Unfortunately, no absolute agreement on terminology about this subject exists, even among feminist scholars. Thus some women of color prefer to call themselves "womanist" scholars to distinguish themselves from the white, upper middle class designation of "feminist." Moreover, many scholars make various linguistic distinctions, some of which may be helpful and some of which may be more obfuscating than necessary. One helpful distinction is made between sex and gender. Whereas *sex* refers to the biological reality of being male or female, *gender* refers to the different ways in which people experience their sexual identity as male or female.[13] We should also emphasize that differences in gender roles are largely dictated by cultural mores that vary from culture to culture. The cultural conventions about gender in North America are not the same as those in Africa or Asia. The concept of gender is culturally determined. A related distinction is between the terms female/male and feminine/masculine. Although the terms are obviously interrelated, the first set refers again to the biological reality of sex while the latter terms refer to gender. This distinction is useful in order to keep in mind that, when discussing questions of sexism, we are most concerned with the broader issues that relate to the way human beings experience their sexual identities, namely, gender bias. Thus sexism is primarily concerned with operative societal stereotypes that reflect gender bias. Common assumptions, such as men do not cry or women do not do well in mathematics or science, reflect gender biases that, from a psychological or biological standpoint, are not accurate. The question of exclusive or inclusive language is most concerned, then, with gender and with the ways we perceive masculine and feminine attributes, attitudes, and behavior.

4. Bishops' Guidelines and the Social Context

The American bishops' own guidelines refer to the societal context that undergirds the concern for language. Three of the five initial statements about the historical context for issuing their guidelines address the wider societal concern for inclusive language (#1). The two that are specifically ecclesial concerns will be considered below, but first I will list the societal concerns.

The first societal concern pointed out by the bishops is that some people have become sensitive to "language which seems to exclude the equality and dignity of each person regardless of race, gender, creed, age, or ability." One should note that the is-

13. See Sandra Schneiders, *Women and the Word: The Gender of God in the New Testament and the Spirituality of Women* (New York: Paulist, 1991) 8–11.

sue of inclusivity is not limited to gender. It embraces ethnic identity, religious beliefs, age, and personal physical and mental abilities.

The second concern pointed out by the bishops is the "noticeable loss of the sense of grammatical gender in American usage of the English language." The third related societal concern is the change in English vocabulary, with the result that "words which once referred to all human beings are increasingly taken as gender specific and, consequently, exclusive."

In these latter two concerns the bishops are acknowledging the fact that language is a dynamic human enterprise that changes with human experience. The meanings of words change over time. Vocabulary shifts with societal changes. Words that once were perceived to be inclusive of all humanity have now become problematic. For example, words like "man," "men," "mankind," "brethren," and "forefathers" once referred to all people regardless of gender, but are now understood more restrictively. Such language shifts need to be taken into account in all areas of contemporary life, including the Church.

In essence, all three of these guidelines are responding to the "signs of the times" in American culture, a stance that reflects Vatican Council II's clarion call for the Church to become aware of and respond to its wider societal context (*Gaudium et spes,* "The Constitution on the Church in the Modern World" #4). Specifics of the Bishops' Guidelines will be included when appropriate in the various sections below.

B. Theological Context

Given this sketch of the larger societal background, I want to turn now to a second context that shapes the issue of inclusivity. The theological rationale for addressing the problem of exclusive language rests upon three foundations: the nature of the mystery of God, the biblical testimony, and the theological underpinnings of the Church's liturgical life. We will examine each of these briefly.

1. The Mystery of God

The overarching theological aspect of issues pertaining to inclusive language may seem so obvious as to be mundane, namely, the mystery of God. This concept, however, is crucial to the discussion. I begin with it here because it is a basic presupposition of the theological context.

At the center of all discussion about theological and liturgical language is the mysterious nature of the one we call God. In the Judeo-Christian tradition God is ultimately *mystery.* Attempts to describe, define, or categorize God always fall short of the reality. God is the utterly "holy one," the totally "other," the mysterious and ineffable source of all life. To speak of God in any language is to search for ways of touching a mystery that is ultimately beyond our full comprehension. I will pursue this in more detail later in relation to references to God. For now it is enough to say that all language struggles to explain that which is ultimately unexplainable in purely rational terms. Perhaps we can let a line from Robert Frost work its magic with regard to this mystery: "We dance 'round a ring and suppose, but the Secret sits in the middle and knows!"

2. Biblical Testimony

The Bible itself mirrors the complexity of the problem of exclusive language. On the one hand, the contextual horizon of the Bible is that of unchallenged patriarchy. One cannot deny the patriarchal dimensions of the Bible, though we will see that it may be less patriarchal than some imagine. Within the limits of human language, metaphor, and social experience, the Bible reflects a culture dominated by patriarchal values and images in which men are predominate and women are subordinate. On the other hand, the Bible's own ethic of liberation versus oppression, seen in both the God of the Exodus and the teaching of Jesus Christ, demands that we go beyond the limitations of prior generations. Within the Bible itself there are exceptions to the cultural norms of patriarchy, especially when applied to the image of God (e.g., Gen 2; Deut 32:18; Isa 42:14; 46:3-4; 66:13; Matt 23:37; Luke 13:34; 15:8-10). I will examine some of these exceptions below. The challenge of the biblical testimony is to find ways in which the more inclusive dimensions of biblical teaching can come to the fore while the more exclusive dimensions are redirected and reinterpreted in a proper framework.

3. Liturgical Underpinnings of the Church

Further impetus for the use of inclusive language comes from the liturgical life of the Church. The Bishops' Guidelines point out two particular ecclesial influences on this issue. The first is that "the introduction of the vernacular into the Church's worship has necessitated English translations of the liturgical books and of sacred Scripture for use in the liturgy" (#1). This reality, in fact, is made all the more complicated by the necessity of designing contemporary English texts not just for the U.S. but also for the English-speaking world. This task is performed by the International Commission on English in the Liturgy (ICEL), headquartered in Washington, D.C. Despite a general impression that inclusive language is a uniquely American phenomenon, my experiences abroad indicate that this is not an accurate appraisal. In an age of rapid communication, it is becoming a concern for the entire English-speaking world and is even making inroads into other languages. Liturgical texts especially often require long and careful consideration before they are authorized for use in public liturgy. Differences of English usage based upon separate English-speaking cultures, as well as different preferences regarding style, make ICEL's job quite complex.[14]

A second ecclesial context pointed out by the bishops is that "impromptu efforts at inclusive language, while pleasing to some, have often offended others who expect a degree of theological precision and linguistic or aesthetic refinement in the public discourse of the liturgy" (#1). This observation summarizes precisely one of my own motivations for writing this handbook. As the bishops

14. Note the controversy over inclusive language created by the English translation of the *Catechism of the Catholic Church* (the so-called universal catechism) as reported in the *NCR* (March 26, 1993) 14. The ensuing discussions delayed its publication in the United States by many months. In the end, when it was finally published in English in June 1994, the translation reverted to exclusive language.

go on to emphasize, the danger is not simply offended ears but the possibility that such impromptu decisions have "unwittingly undermined essentials of Catholic doctrine." This is an implicit recognition of the power of language. At the heart of the ecclesial context is the fact that the very nature of liturgy is public and communal. Indeed the Greek root of the word indicates this (*leitourgon* from *laos* ["people"] + *ergos* ["work"]). Liturgy is by nature a group activity. It is not a platform for one's particular theological views to be proclaimed, yet liturgy must also not serve as a vehicle for oppression by fostering exclusivity and inequality. The issue of inclusive language, whether we like it or not, is not simply a passing fad. Rather it is an urgent issue of theological import and social justice and one that calls for responsible action.

An even more essential aspect of the liturgical life of the Church is the nature of the worshiping community as a Eucharistic communion of believers. The Eucharist is the primary locus of our unity as the Body of Christ. Two quotes from our tradition, one biblical and one ecclesial, will illustrate this point well. St. Paul writes to the Corinthian community, a community beset by serious factionalism and division, the following words: "The cup of blessing that we bless, is it not a sharing in the blood of Christ? The bread that we break, is it not a sharing in the body of Christ? Because there is one bread, we who are many are one body, for we all partake of the one bread" (1 Cor 10:16-17).

This image of Eucharistic unity, along with many other biblical images, is picked up in Vatican II by the famous passage that calls the Eucharist the source and summit of the Church's life of prayer.

> The liturgy is . . . the high point towards which the activity of the church is directed, and, simultaneously, the source from which all its power flows out. For the point of apostolic work is that all those who have become children of God through faith and baptism can assemble together in order to praise God in the midst of the church, to share in the sacrifice, and to eat the Lord's supper (*Sacrosanctum concilium*, "Constitution on the Sacred Liturgy" #10).[15]

15. See also the extensive image of unity developed in *Lumen Gentium*, "The Dogmatic Constitution on the Church," no. 7. The quotation is from

When we gather as "church" for liturgy, especially for the Eucharist, our words, our posture, our gestures, our actions should reflect the deep union of *all* who are baptized into Christ Jesus. All are redeemed equally by the same Christ. Our liturgy should reflect and embody this deeper unity as a Eucharistic community. The American Roman Catholic bishops have shown their willingness to begin addressing the issue of liturgical language by commissioning new biblical translations and a revision of the liturgical books.[16] Recently completed are new translations of the New Testament and Psalms of *The New American Bible*,[17] which prepare the way for revisions in the current Lectionary. Revisions of the Eucharistic Prayers and other parts of the Sacramentary are also in progress. All will be prepared with some sensitivity to inclusive language, though results are likely to be unsatisfactory to many people. Some will feel this action by the bishops is grudgingly too little and too late. Others will see their stance as an unfortunate yielding to excessive feminist concerns. I think the fact that progress is being made in sensitivity to language, however slowly, is a sign that the issue is taken seriously by the American hierarchy and that changes will be made cautiously.

C. Local Context

The third major context is the local level. The larger societal and ecclesial contexts provide a backdrop for what immediately touches most people in their daily lives—the local context of each worshiping community. Each member of the worshiping commu-

---

Norman P. Tanner, ed., *Decrees of the Ecumenical Councils* (London: Sheed & Ward; Washington: Georgetown University, 1990) 2:823. One notes that Tanner's translation of the official documents purposefully attempts to be as inclusive as context allows.

16. The Canadian bishops have also addressed this issue. See *The National Bulletin on Liturgy* (CCCB) 25 (1992) 131. The entire issue is on the Lectionary, accompanied by good bibliographical references and a summary of major issues on the revision of the Canadian Lectionary.

17. See the bibliographical information in the Table of Abbreviations. This translation was fully approved by the NCCB for liturgical use in November, 1991.

nity is responsible for manifesting a sensitivity to those who are present at worship. This responsibility with regard to inclusive language is best enunciated in the general principle published by ICEL in *Eucharistic Prayers*: "Both sound theology and pastoral sensitivity require that the language used in all liturgical texts, as well as in all other aspects of liturgy, for example, preaching, should not only permit but indeed facilitate the full participation of women in the worship of the Church."[18]

This position was recently reinforced by the Bishops' Guidelines on inclusive language, as the following two citations indicate.

> The language of biblical texts for liturgical use should be suitably and faithfully adapted for proclamation and should facilitate the full, conscious and active participation of all members of the church, women and men, in worship (#13).

> Language which addresses and refers to the worshiping community ought not use words or phrases which deny the common dignity of all the baptized (#17).

Liturgy, then, should be a vehicle for inclusivity. Liturgy should uphold the dignity of all human beings, male and female. The bishops also point out that the Word of God by its very nature is universally inclusive because it is "addressed to all peoples, men and women" (#14). Thus, all who serve as liturgical ministers in whatever capacity are urged to use inclusive language in public worship.

In summary, these three contexts—societal, theological, and local—form the background and impetus for incorporating inclusive language into the liturgical life of the Church. The following principles and practical guidelines are offered as a means of identifying the various situations in which inclusive language may or may not be employed.[19]

---

18. *Eucharistic Prayers* (Washington, D.C.: ICEL, 1980) 66.

19. These guidelines are specifically offered for the English language and do not presume to address the issue of exclusivity in other languages (e.g., French or Spanish). The principles delineated in this book do not necessarily apply in the same manner to other languages because of their own unique complexities.

Chapter II.

The Principles of Inclusive Language

The principles of inclusive language can be divided into general principles and applied principles. We will take each in turn.

A. THREE GENERAL PRINCIPLES

Before delineating specific principles for inclusive language, we need to state three general principles that are foundational for what follows.

(1) The uppermost goal of any attempt to communicate the Word of God in an inclusive way should be fidelity to the biblical text as a canonical text. The meaning of the canon (from the Greek *kanōn* = "norm, rule") is that of inspired literature, valued for its normative function in the life of the Church. The biblical readings used in liturgy should reflect the exegetical and linguistic decisions that communicate the Word of God faithfully in the original text. This principle, in fact, is one of two primary guidelines on biblical translations promulgated by the bishops (#7), and it is given primacy over that of "respect for the nature of the liturgical assembly," when conflict or ambiguity exists between the two principles.

(2) Public presentation of the Word of God must not be confused with the way one might reflect upon it in personal devotion. The public communication of the Word requires greater sensitivity to language than does the private study of the Bible for one's own spiritual enrichment. This too is a guideline in the bishops' document: "Because their immediate purposes are somewhat different, texts translated for public proclamation in the liturgy may differ in some respects from those translations which are meant solely for academic study, private reading or *lectio divina*" (#12). A profound difference exists between liturgy and the ancient tradition of *lectio divina*, private and prayerful reflection on the Word of God.[20] Thus, decisions about linguistic changes should reflect a concern for how the worshiping community in a public setting will receive the Word of God proclaimed to them.

(3) Readings should never be changed linguistically on impulse at the last minute. Readers, presiders, preachers, and liturgy planning teams should always prepare the biblical texts *in advance* so that sound linguistic decisions can be made from a nuanced understanding of the texts. Nothing is more embarrassing and annoying than to hear a reader begin a reading and change perceived exclusive words in it, only to box himself or herself into a corner with almost nonsensical or repetitive language. With the current approved biblical translations that are permitted for liturgy,[21] there is no excuse for last minute preparation.

These three general principles undergird the following applied principles. The purpose of this next section is both to provide the rationale for appropriate changes that have been or can be made in the biblical text, and to point out the inherent pitfalls this process can entail.

---

20. An accessible, succinct introduction to this ancient prayerful practice is Karl A. Schultz, *"Lectio Divina,"* BToday 31 (1993) 197–199.

21. Three translations of the Bible were originally approved by the NCCB for use in Roman Catholic liturgies, *The Jerusalem Bible*, the NABRNT, and the Catholic edition of the *NRSV*. See the *Bishops' Committee on the Liturgy Newsletter/NCCB* 23 (January 1987) 3, and 28 (May 1992) 17. However, in October 1994 the Vatican withdrew permission to use the *NRSV* in public worship. For an overview of this development see chapter four.

B. Applied Principles

The applied principles of inclusive language in biblical texts may be divided into two areas: language about people or persons and language about God, with special reference to the persons of the Trinity. These are known as horizontal and vertical inclusive language. We will also include a final section on the importance of context.

1. References to People, Persons

Many contemporary biblical translations that remain in use, including the current Lectionary, employ gender exclusive terms where none exists in the original text. In such cases changes should be made to reflect the more exact intention of the biblical text. Fortunately, as we pointed out above, several new translations of the Bible that have recently appeared and that have deliberately employed inclusive language wherever possible are available. These should be consulted for suggested ways of handling specific biblical texts.

Terms such as man, mankind, men, forefathers, brothers, brethren, etc., were once understood generically as well as with reference to human males (cf. Bishops' Guidelines #18). This situation has changed in recent years. Even contemporary dictionaries note that the words "man" or "men" no longer serve appropriately to designate the human race.[22] More importantly from a theological perspective, one should note that the term "man" as it is used in many biblical texts was used to translate *adam* (Hebrew) or *anthrōpos* (Greek) or *homo* (Latin), words that actually refer to the "human being" rather than the male gender. Often such exclusive terms can be replaced validly by other words that are more inclusive, such as: sisters and brothers, daughters and sons, family, ancestors, men and women, humanity, human race, humankind, people, persons, etc.[23]

22. For example, *The American Heritage Dictionary*, 2d ed. (Boston: Houghton Mifflin, 1982) 761, and *The Oxford English Dictionary* (Oxford: Clarendon, 1933) 6:99.
23. This section is based entirely on *Eucharistic Prayers* (p. 66) where a more complete listing of possible terms is included.

In many cases, such as in the Pauline letters, the form of address used ("brothers") properly addresses the entire Christian community and thus should be translated "sisters and brothers" or something similar.[24] Scholars are generally agreed on this principle, and it is another of the guidelines for the revision of the Lectionary. However, care must be taken to determine the *context*. Sometimes, the address is strictly meant to apply to the male members of the community or to male characters in the biblical text (e.g., Acts 7:1; Phlm 20; 1 and 2 Tim; Titus). Care should be taken not to confuse a historically accurate biblical term with one that is patently sexist. Thus, for example, reference to human kings cannot simply be replaced by "kings and queens," though a possible substitution for "kings" might be "rulers." In the ancient world, queens did not normally play the same type of role that kings played. This statement is particularly true for ancient Israel, and it is not compromised by scriptural examples of women who reigned as queens, e.g., Sheba, the non-Israelite ruler of the Sabeans (1 Kgs 10:1-10, 13); Jezebel, the Phoenician wife of Ahab (1 and 2 Kgs); or Athaliah, the daughter of Jezebel (2 Kgs 8:18; 11:1-20). The contexts of these passages indicate that the inherent abilities and forceful personalities of these women enabled them to reach such positions of power. In the biblical world they are the exception rather than the norm.[25] The kings in Israelite tradition played a very important role in covenantal contexts and in the embodiment of the people in their relationship to God.

In addition, the phrase "sons of God" cannot always be replaced by "sons and daughters of God" or "children of God." One must ask whether the phrase refers to the sons of God who are divine beings (cf. Pss 29:1; 89:7 *REB/NAB*; Gen 6:2, 4; Job 1:6) or angels (Dan 3:25, 29), or the children of God who are thus both men and women (compare Ps 34:12 "children" *NAB* and *Psalms* with "sons" in Ps 34:11 *JB*; Hos 1:10 *NEB*; Rom 8:14

---

24. I find it curious that, despite their acknowledgement of this position, the revisers of the *NABRNT* chose not to translate *adelphoi* with "brothers and sisters" (p. 53). Compare the translation of "brothers and sisters" or "friends" in the *REB* and the *NRSV*.

25. For an excellent treatment of other Old Testament texts from a feminist perspective, see the books of Phyllis Trible listed in the bibliography.

NABRNT). Yet, phrases such as "the sons of men" (= human beings) or "the sons of Israel" (= Israelites), when not referring to males (as in Gen 42:5 *NRSV*, Israel's sons), should be properly translated by inclusive language (e.g., "children of the earth" or "human beings," "children of Israel" or "Israelites"), since the expression, "sons of . . ." is the common Hebrew way of designating belonging to a class of persons. Another problem is posed by the use of singular relative pronouns. Although some experts have recommended the replacement of the singular number with plural (e.g., "he who" replaced by "they who"), this action may not be the best course with regard to *all* Scripture readings. In general, this is an acceptable substitution and is one of the guiding principles of the committee revising the Lectionary. For example, we can make a comparison between the *RSV* and the *NRSV* translations of Luke 9:23.

> "If *any man* would come after me, let *him* deny *himself* and take up *his* cross daily and follow me" *(RSV).*

> "If *any* want to become my followers, let *them* deny *themselves* and take up *their* cross daily and follow me" *(NRSV).*

But in some instances such a substitution could result in a distortion of the text. For example, the thought of John's Gospel relies heavily on the notion of the individual and his or her relationship to Jesus and thus to God (e.g., John 6:35-65 and 15:1-27). To replace the singular with the plural blurs this theological insight (see the *NRSV* rendering of John 15:5), although some suggest that the Johannine text switches between singular and plural verb forms often enough to question this necessity. The same principle might also apply to some of the psalms, such as the individual laments where the theology of lament is rooted in the individual (not the community as a whole) crying out with whole heart to God in times of difficulty (Pss 3–7; 22; 26; 28; 51; etc.), although there is surely a close connection between individual and communal prayer in the Hebrew tradition. On the other hand, a phrase like "Happy the man who" (Ps 1:1) is not meant to be exclusive to the male gender and can easily be rendered by the singular ("Happy the one who") or by the plural ("Happy those who").[26]

26. The Hebrew word *'ish* used in Ps 1:1 normally means "man" (male) but can also be used as here in the generic sense of "human person."

One may be comforted to know that such issues are not only found in ecclesial contexts. Even in secular literature, substituting the plural for the singular is not always considered appropriate in every instance. For example, the authors' guidelines for one publishing company state: "It would be wrong to pluralize in contexts stressing a one-to-one relationship. In such cases, either using the expression *he* or *she* or alternating *he* and *she*, as appropriate, will be acceptable" (no emphasis added).[27] Of course, one must also avoid the tedious repetition of such terminology, but there are usually ways of working out alternate phrasing.

A further instance of blurring the meaning of the text in an effort to avoid exclusive language can be to maintain the third person but make it generic. One scholar has pointed out that the *NRSV* rendering of Luke 14:27 distorts the text.[28] The translation, "Whoever does not carry *the* cross and follow me cannot be my disciple," makes it appear that we are called to carry the cross of Jesus, where the Greek text explicitly refers to the disciple's own cross. The fear is that this can inadvertently reinforce an inappropriate "Jesus-did-it-all-for-me Christianity" that is already prevalent among many Bible-toting Christians.

Another alternative that biblical translators turn to is to switch from the third person to second person in order to avoid exclusive language, provided it does not alter the sense of the text. This also is a guiding principle of those revising the Lectionary. An illustration is the saying in Matthew 18:6 where in the *NRSV* the third person singular he/him/his has been replaced by the second person: "If *any of you* put a stumbling block before one of these little ones who believe in me, it would be better for *you* if a great millstone were fastened around *your* neck and *you* were drowned in the depth of the sea." Inclusivity is achieved without detriment

27. See *Guidelines for Equal Treatment of the Sexes in McGraw-Hill Book Company Publications* (New York: McGraw-Hill, n.d.) 8–9. Virtually all publishers now have authors' guidelines regarding inclusive language.

28. Walter Wink, "The New RSV: The Best Translation, Halfway There," *Christian Century* 107 (1990) 831. For an explanation of how the *NRSV* was put together, see Bruce M. Metzger et al., *The Making of the New Revised Standard Version of the Bible* (Grand Rapids: Eerdmans, 1991). For a brief review of the *NABRNT*, see "The Good News on 'Man,' " *Commonweal* 114 (April 24, 1987) 228–229.

to the meaning of the text and with a rather moderate change of words. In parables and stories the characters identified should be maintained in their proper gender and referred to in the proper way. This principle is specifically enunciated in the Bishops' Guidelines (#20). Although there is an abundance of male characters used in such stories, some are alternated with stories with female characters or even feminine imagery (e.g., Luke 13:18-21; 15:1-10; cf. Matt 13:31-33), which should be utilized to their fullest extent when the texts come in the liturgical cycle.

Texts That Denigrate the Status of Women

A special case of texts referring to persons is found in passages that appear to denigrate women. Most galling to many women is having to sit through a Sunday reading that, at least to modern ears, seems to denigrate women. Some biblical texts seem to presume the inferiority of women and their natural subjection to men (e.g., 1 Cor 14:34-36; Eph 5:21-24; Col 3:18). One hopes that the revision of the Lectionary may excise some of these texts and replace them with more palatable readings for a public setting. But I would raise three concerns about this course of action.

The first concern is that these readings may or may not be as exclusive as they first appear.[29] In the New Testament the writings of St. Paul and the Pauline tradition are often singled out for a troublesome and almost irredeemable attitude toward women. Examples are abundant. In his First Letter to the Corinthians Paul speaks of the man as the "head" of the woman, the need for a woman to have her head veiled, and the view that woman was created "for the sake of man" (1 Cor 11:2-16). Elsewhere in the same letter Paul calls it "shameful for a woman to speak in church" (1 Cor 14:34-35). In making a comparison of the relationship between Christ and the Church and husband and wife in marriage, two letters of the Pauline tradition seem to set the husband above the wife in terms of authority and obedience (Eph 5:21-33; Col 3:18-21).

Unfortunately, such readings falling on modern ears communicate ideas that are not necessarily part of the legitimate back-

---

29. See, for example, the exposition of Eph 5:23 in John Paul II's apostolic letter, *Mulieris Dignitatem* (1988) no. 24.

ground of the reading. Sometimes these readings are used as a legitimation of the subjugation and even abuse of women by men, as if women (and children) are somehow chattel for men. This is not a valid use of the readings, nor is it the intention in the biblical text.

Although space limitations prohibit our full consideration of this matter, my concern is that we may be too hasty to write them off as irrelevant because they do not conform to our own preconceptions. Sometimes texts that sound misogynistic may or may not be so. At other times we may simply need to recognize the historical and cultural limitations of such texts. In fact, some passages that *seem* to be hopelessly exclusive in nature are not, as careful exposition of the text would show.[30] Modern commentators on such troublesome passages should be consulted. In addition, the newer, more inclusive biblical translations may clear up some of the difficulties by their choice of words and explanatory notes.

A second concern is about the danger of trying to rewrite history. The temptation is often strong to want to sweep away bad memories. For instance, some would like to forget that the Holocaust (the Shoah), the Nazi attempt to exterminate the Jews, ever took place.[31] Jewish writers especially remind us of the need to *remember* precisely so that such a horrendous act will never be repeated in history. As regards difficult biblical readings, rather than excluding them altogether from the Lectionary or altering them beyond their actual meaning, could they not be seen as an opportunity by the homilist (also by the liturgical planners) to proclaim a message about the nature of Sacred Scripture, the cultural horizons of those who wrote the Scriptures, or the complexity of God's Word as it is applied to various cultures and people through the ages? A congregation might learn a great deal from a careful exposition of such difficult passages. Some scholars directly argue that these passages are important to preserve because

30. See the sensitive treatment of controversial Pauline passages in Brendan Byrne, *Paul and the Christian Woman* (Collegeville, Minn.: The Liturgical Press, 1988).

31. There are even books and articles being published that deny the historicity of this atrocity. See Walter Reich, "Erasing the Holocaust," *New York Times Book Review* (July 11, 1993) 1, 31, 33–34.

of their testimony to ingrained misogyny over the centuries. Attitudes found in them are a part of our historical heritage. Another example of this heritage might be the issue of slavery. Contrary to being condemned in the Bible, in both Testaments slavery is presumed as a cultural institution.[32] Does this mean we should not read any of those passages about slaves just because we now live in an enlightened era when slavery is recognized as an outrage against human dignity? We can hardly act in such a fashion without affecting detrimentally our history. I suggest that such biblically problematic passages should not be cast out of sight. They serve as reminders of the power of the Word as a two-edged sword (Heb 4:12) that at times led historically to exclusive and oppressive human conditions as well as to salvation.

The third concern is probably the most important. An inherent danger of excluding unfavorable biblical readings is that we will create a "canon within a canon." This process can lead to the tendency to pick and choose the readings we *want* to hear while ignoring the ones we *need* to hear. This is not to say that the Lectionary should include readings clearly inappropriate for public worship. The public setting is naturally different from the private one. But those who might wish to exclude troublesome biblical readings altogether because they do not fit into our modern conceptions open themselves to a highly selective form of Christianity. When placed in the context of the *entire* canon of Sacred Scripture, any reading can be softened or balanced by other biblical teachings. For these three reasons I think we must be cautious about the urge to hide readings we find embarrassing or oppressive.

In sum, references to people in many biblical texts should be as inclusive as possible. While some texts will remain problematic, the ability to change references to human beings in these texts is relatively straightforward when compared to the next area—language referring to God.

2. *References to God*

Nothing is probably more controversial about inclusive language than how it applies to God. Many people understand well

32. For an overview of the biblical and cultural data see Carolyn Osiek, "Slavery in the Second Testament World," *BTB* 22 (1992) 174–179.

the need for sensitivity when referring to *people* who might take offense at exclusive expressions, but how can we tamper with language about *God?* This sensitive area is a theological minefield fraught with booby traps. We will try to tiptoe our way through this "no (wo)man's land"! The topic will be examined according to four categories: the nature of God-talk, patriarchal language in titles, feminine imagery for God, and the Trinity.

A. THE NATURE OF GOD-TALK

Of utmost importance is to understand the nature of God-talk, that is, words we use to describe, define, and understand God. Most biblical language is by nature metaphorical. Language about God is by necessity analogical. These two factors help maintain the proper perspective in approaching questions of inclusive/exclusive language with regard to God. I pointed out above (p. 14) the essential nature of God as mystery. No single biblical image or metaphor can capture the full reality and mystery we name "God." The limitations of human language (even the Word of God in human words) to express the incomprehensibility of God must always be acknowledged.[33]

The *Catechism of the Catholic Church* also recognizes the limitations of human language with regard to descriptions of God when it notes:

> God transcends all creatures. We must therefore continually purify our language of everything in it that is limited, image-bound or imperfect, if we are not to confuse our image of God— "the inexpressible, the incomprehensible, the invisible, the ungraspable"—with our human representations. Our human words always fall short of the mystery of God.[34]

---

33. See especially Elizabeth A. Johnson, "The Incomprehensibility of God and the Image of God Male and Female," *TS* 45 (1984) 441–465, which provides the kernel of the argumentation for her book, *She Who Is,* listed in the bibliography.

34. *Catechism of the Catholic Church* (Libreria Editrice Vaticana, 1994) no. 42, quoting from the *Liturgy of St. John Chrysostom.* Paragraph number 43 continues in the same vein while emphasizing that the limitations of human modes of expression do not prevent us from making contact with God.

For some feminists even the word "God" itself is an inappropriate term because it deceives us into thinking we can actually name that which is ineffable. Thus some prefer to use the designation, "G-d"[35] in place of the traditional term. While I applaud the efforts of feminist theologians to remind us of the ultimate mystery of God, I confess that I do not find this substitute term helpful, not the least because it is unpronounceable. In the biblical tradition we already have an unpronounceable and mysterious name for God in the Tetragrammaton (the four-letter Hebrew designation, YHWH [= I am who I am], for the God of Israel; Exod 3:14), which undergirds the New Testament designation of Jesus in John's Gospel as "I AM" (John 8:24, 28, 58; 13:19). Precisely because it was the ineffable, unpronounceable name did the Israelites substitute the designation "Lord" (Hebrew = *adonai*) for the sacred name. What is helpful, though, is the reminder that traditional labels for God represent analogical language that should not be confused with literal images. Elizabeth Johnson is a theologian who has written extensively and eloquently on the "incomprehensibility" of God. She states, "The incomprehensibility of God makes it entirely appropriate, at times even preferable, to speak about God in nonpersonal supra-personal terms."[36] This statement refers to the limitations of employing masculine imagery for God. At the same time she warns that merely employing feminine imagery for God can fall into the same trap as traditional patriarchal imagery and become a literal way of viewing God.

Certainly an aspect of the biblical tradition is to speak of God in nonpersonal ways. Psalm 18:1-2 is a good example of a series of designations strung together like pearls on a chain, each pearl emphasizing one aspect of God or another:

I love you, O LORD, my strength.
The LORD is my rock, my fortress, and my deliverer,
  my God, my rock in whom I take refuge,
  my shield, and the horn of my salvation, my stronghold.

35. Schüssler Fiorenza, *But She Said*, 6, quoting the work of Rebecca S. Chopp, *The Power to Speak: Feminism, Language, God* (New York: Crossroad, 1989).

36. Johnson, *She Who Is*, 45.

The psalms frequently mention God as a "rock" (Ps 18:31, 46; 19:14; 28:1, etc.), and often God is referred to as "the Holy One of Israel" (2 Kgs 19:22; Isa 1:4; 5:19, 24) or simply "the Holy One" (Isa 10:17; Hos 11:9), and a host of other images (Redeemer, Creator, etc.). Referring to the holiness of God is a way of emphasizing that God is totally other, distinct from humanity. Some would see in the nonpersonal attributes that the Bible uses of God a way out of the impasse of exclusive language. But speaking of God only in terms of traits is also an inadequate alternative because it reduces God to a series of impersonal characteristic attitudes or actions. The upshot of this discussion is to recognize the inherent limitations of *all language* with regard to God and to remember the metaphorical and analogical nature of all God-talk. Nevertheless, in a discussion of inclusive language, we must explore the limits of patriarchal imagery and possible alternatives within the biblical tradition.

B. Patriarchal Language in Titles

The problem with patriarchal language regarding God is summarized by Elizabeth Johnson: "Speech about God in the exclusive and literal terms of the patriarch is a tool of subtle conditioning that operates to debilitate women's sense of dignity, power, and self-esteem."[37] What does one do in the face of such an evaluation? I believe it is possible to retain traditional terminology while supplementing it with a broader, more diverse set of images. Of course, some feminists object to the notion of supplementation or complementarity as perpetuating patriarchal dominance while only paying lip service to valid feminist concerns. Yet the dictionary definition of supplement is "to complete a thing, make up for a deficiency, or extend or strengthen the whole."[38] In this sense, supplementing the tradition is restoring to a rightful place that which has equal validity and was lost, shunned, or ignored in the past. Such supplementation does not automatically lead to secondary status but to a restoration for the sake of improvement.

Despite the attempts at alternatives made in the experimental *Inclusive Language Lectionary*[39] of some years ago, it is prefer-

37. Ibid., 38.
38. *American Heritage Dictionary*, 1221.
39. *An Inclusive Language Lectionary*, 3 vols. (Atlanta: John Knox, 1984–

able at the present time to maintain such biblical titles as "Son of God," "Son of Man," "son of David," "son of Abraham," etc., with reference to Jesus Christ. Some of these should be obvious, but one question arises with the curious phrase "Son of Man." This title requires a little explanation. The expression "son of man" is found in the Old Testament, especially in Ezekiel. There the expression clearly is not a title but a designation in normal Hebrew fashion of Ezekiel as a human being in contrast to God, the utterly holy one, who calls him to be a prophet. Thus the *NRSV* translates the phrase as "mortal." Another example is the famous line from Psalm 8:4:

> What is *man* that thou art mindful of him,
> the *son of man* that you keep him in mind?

This is an example of Hebrew poetic parallelism in which two parallel lines say the same thing in different words. A more inclusive translation is the *NRSV*:

> What are *human beings* that you are mindful of them,
> *mortals* that you care for them? (See also *Psalms*.)

The real problem with the latter inclusive translation arises with the next verse of the psalm, which is directly applied in Hebrews 2:9 to Jesus Christ. Maintaining the translation with the plural obscures the Christological import that the "son of man" who is "made a little lower than God" and "crowned with glory and honor" receives in Hebrews and in the Christian tradition.

Elsewhere problems can arise when Old Testament passages are read through Christian eyes for Christological or messianic meaning. Other illustrations can be found in Daniel 7:13 ("one like a son of man"), where the expression "son of man" is almost a title, and with other phrases emphasizing sonship, lordship, or servanthood, such as Psalm 2:7 ("you are my son; today I have begotten you"), Psalm 110:1 ("The LORD says to my lord"), and

---

1985). For an explanation of the rationale of the proposed translations of this Lectionary, see Patrick D. Miller, Jr., "The Inclusive Language Lectionary," *TToday* 41 (1984) 26–33. One example of the strong criticism that this experimental Lectionary elicited is Elizabeth Achtemeier, "The Translator's Dilemma: Inclusive Language," *Interpretation* 38 (1984) 64–66.

the songs of the Suffering Servant in Isaiah 42 and 53. In cases such as these, the Bishops' Guidelines remind biblical translators of the necessity to safeguard the Christological teaching inherent in them (#29).

In addition to "Son of Man" and "Son of God," we should maintain the use of "Father," "King," "Lord," etc., with reference to God or to Jesus. The meaning of some of these ancient titles or designations is not always apparent even to biblical scholars. Given their historical and theological importance, they should not be changed lightly. I will discuss some of these images below.[40]

A special case is also found in the expression "kingdom of God" (or "kingdom of heaven"), which scholars agree was central to the teaching of Jesus. Some object to the expression because of its masculine emphasis on "king" when the Greek expression *(hē basileia tou theou)* can properly be translated "reign of God" or "rule of God" (Mark 1:15 and Matt 13:24, *NABRNT*). But a caution is in order here also. To translate the expression solely as God's rule or reign, in the sense of a *temporal* expression or an aspect of God's perspective, is to overlook the *spatial* dimension present in the notion as it at times is portrayed in the Gospels. The kingdom sometimes represents a place as well as a statement about God's reign (Matt 26:29). Thus the kingdom of God can be "entered" (Mark 10:15; Matt 5:20; 7:21; 18:3; 19:23-24) or one can be "locked out" of it (Matt 23:13). Moreover the concept is also connected with the Son of Man coming as a "king" for judgment (Matt 25:31, 34). Both senses of the concept, temporal (or as an aspect) and spatial, ought to be preserved in our usage.

This discussion has thus far emphasized problems that arise with the extensive patriarchal imagery found in the Bible and attempts to change it in wholesale fashion. One should not get the impression that these are the only biblical images available. Due recognition of the exceptions in Scripture to such male-oriented terminology should be recognized and utilized to their fullest extent (e.g., Gen 1:27; Luke 15:8-10; Deut 32:18; Isa 42:14; 46:3-4; 66:13; Matt 23:37; Luke 13:34). Now I will examine some of these

---

40. One notes the reinstatement of "Lord" as an optional reading in volume three (*Readings for Year C*) of *An Inclusive Language Lectionary* (National Council of Christian Churches, 1985) 6.

images briefly to indicate the breadth of alternative imagery that is sometimes used in the Bible.

C. FEMININE IMAGERY FOR GOD

The first passage that should give us some pause with regard to masculine and feminine imagery is in the Genesis story of creation.

> So God created humankind *(adam)* in his image,
> in the image of God he created them;
> male and female he created them (Gen 1:27).

Despite the difficulty of rendering this verse adequately in English (as seen in the masculine pronouns that remain), the text indicates that human beings in their maleness *and* femaleness reflect the very image of God, both male and female.

Two observations about this passage are important. First, the text does not mean that God is androgynous, that is, male/female, but that both male and female persons mirror the divine image. Attempts to see both God and Goddess in this text are not consistent with Old Testament faith. Second, the context of the reading shows that the purpose of the text is not primarily to show equality of the sexes but to show how *both* male and female are creatures created by God and given dominion over the earth (Gen 1:28), each reflecting in their persons the image of God. Neither one *separately* can fully reflect the image of God except *in relation* to the other, for both equally reflect the image of God. That the Hebrew tradition even within its patriarchal worldview could acknowledge that the personhood of God is reflected in both female and male human creatures is important. It should at least remind us not to be too quick to pigeonhole God in our preferred gender categories. Females mirror the divine image as well as males.

More subtle feminine imagery emerges from another part of the Hebrew tradition. For example, when God is called "the one who gave you birth" (Deut 32:18; Num 11:12), the text evokes the image of a woman in labor. This image appears several times in the Old Testament. The Book of Isaiah provides the primary texts excerpted below.

> For a long time I have held my peace,
>   I have kept still and restrained myself;
> now I will cry out *like a woman in labor,*
>   I will gasp and pant (Isa 42:14).
> Listen to me, O house of Jacob,
>   all the remnant of the house of Israel,
> who have been *borne* by me from your birth,
>   *carried from the womb;*
> even to your old age I am he,
>   even when you turn gray I will carry you.
> I have made, and I will bear;
>   I will carry and will save (Isa 46:3-4).

The latter passage shows some mixed imagery, combining general creation vocabulary with that of childbirth. Nonetheless, both passages clearly compare God to a woman who gives birth to a child, caring for the child throughout its life (see also Isa 45:10).

Perhaps the most famous passages comparing God to a mother are those found elsewhere in Isaiah. Isaiah speaks of God as a tender mother ready to give comfort in times of need: "As a mother comforts her child, so I will comfort you" (Isa 66:13). Or who cannot be impressed by this evocative image of tender motherly care:

> Can a woman forget her nursing child,
>   or show no compassion for the child of her womb?
> Even these may forget,
>   yet I will not forget you (Isa 49:15).

The notion of God as mother is indeed a moving image from the biblical tradition, and one that can rightly serve as a balance to overused masculine and father imagery. But one must also notice that the language employed by these texts is that of *simile* (God is *like* . . .). To compare God to a woman in labor is one thing; to label God "mother" or to address God directly as "mother" is not found in the Bible. At the same time the Old Testament also employs the language of simile when speaking of God as a male (e.g., Isa 42:13, God is *like* a soldier and a warrior). Lest we think of feminine imagery as the only tender aspects of God-talk, we should note Psalm 103:13, which also uses a simile of the compassionate father for God:

> As a father has compassion for his children,
> so the LORD has compassion for those who fear him.

But in addition the Old Testament uses more direct language for God as father and husband (e.g., Deut 32:6; Ps 89:26; Jer 31:9; Hos 2:16; 3:1; Mal 2:10; Sir 51:10; cf. Exod 4:22; Hos 11:1). For example, the Book of Isaiah records:

> For you are our *father,*
> though Abraham does not know us
> and Israel does not acknowledge us;
> you, O LORD, are our *father;*
> our Redeemer from of old is your name (Isa 63:16).

Father language is also used in covenantal contexts as in the relationship between the king (e.g., David) and God: "I will be a father to him, and he shall be a son to me" (2 Sam 7:14). The complexity of this biblical material indicates that one cannot reach quick solutions about how best to describe God in anthropomorphic language (that is, reflecting human features). While masculine imagery certainly dominates the Scriptures, it is not exclusively so. While feminine imagery is employed, such language is not as frequent or as direct as masculine imagery. Many feminists would argue that the very language of the Bible itself is predetermined by a biased patriarchal society. From a modern perspective that may be so, but the Old Testament originated in an environment where female deities abounded (e.g., Ishtar, Astarte, among others) and where the opportunity to express fundamental statements about God in feminine terms existed. The use of feminine similes testifies to the multifaceted way of viewing God, even if the predominant image remains masculine. I would argue for the need to rediscover and to employ in appropriate ways feminine imagery for God while at the same time not jettisoning important traditional masculine imagery.

The New Testament also contains some passages evocative of feminine imagery. In the context of bemoaning the unwillingness of Jerusalem to heed God's messengers who have been sent to it, both Matthew and Luke record how Jesus compared himself to a mother hen: "How often have I desired to gather your children together as a hen gathers her brood under her wings, and you were not willing!" (Matt 23:37; Luke 13:34).

In short, while the lion's share of the Bible operates out of a patriarchal view of God with male dominated imagery, there are other strands of tradition that can be validly used to provide some balance in the context of our modern sensitivities. We should not gloss over the feminine imagery that is found in the Bible itself. As the Bishops' Guidelines specifically state:

> Feminine imagery in the original language of the biblical texts should not be obscured or replaced by the use of masculine imagery in English translations, e.g., Wisdom literature (#28).

I will discuss the special case of Wisdom literature below. For now my primary point is that the Judeo-Christian biblical tradition does have a more diversified way of speaking of God than we have generally allowed into our consciousness.

D. THE TRINITY

Concerning Trinitarian language, I believe it is best to maintain traditional usage, despite a popular practice to do otherwise. Among some it has become common to use a substitute Trinitarian formula such as "in the name of the Creator, Redeemer, and Sanctifier (or Sustainer)" or "the Creator, the Word made flesh, and the Spirit of love" (among other alternatives) in order to avoid masculine imagery for God. Such a practice is inappropriate and represents a seriously flawed theology. It reduces the mystery of the Trinity to mere *functions,* a practice that distorts the personhood and relationality of God. The rationale for this position requires further explanation.

In the course of discussing the three persons of the Trinity I will offer seven reasons for preserving at this time the traditional Trinitarian language. The first three reasons are general in nature while the fourth specifically applies to the first person of the Trinity. The remaining reasons apply to the Son and Holy Spirit.

(1) The language of the traditional Trinitarian formula antedates any fully developed Trinitarian theology (e.g., Matt 28:19; cf. 1 Cor 12:4-6; 2 Cor 13:13; 2 Thess 2:13-14; 1 Pet 1:2) but became foundational in the development of that theology. This assertion does not mean that the New Testament evinces a fully developed Trinitarian theology such as developed in the later centuries, but that the essential seeds of that theology are present

in the biblical data. The canonical status of the Bible places limits on the degree to which we would want to transgress the biblical teaching, although later theological views are not restricted to the biblical teaching.

(2) In the Christian tradition, the act of creation is not limited to the Father, nor is the act of redemption limited to the Son, or sanctification limited to the Spirit. Each person of the Trinity participates in these various divine actions, yet they flow from the oneness of God. God acts as one even while three distinct persons are said to share fully the one identity.

(3) The mystery of the Trinity is not only a mystery about the identity of God but also about God as a *relational* being. Maintaining the distinctiveness of the divine persons is essential to expressing their interrelationship, which in turn has implications for ourselves as relational beings. Elizabeth Johnson has effectively described the situation in which we find ourselves with regard to Trinitarian language. She writes that the difficulty is that "we have forgotten what was clear to early Christian thinkers, namely, that Father and Son are names that designate relationships rather than an essence in itself, and that as applied to God they, like all human finite names, are subject to the negation of the rule of analogy."[41] These words occur in the context of deemphasizing the overly literal identification of patriarchal imagery for the Trinity, but they also remind us of the essential nature of God as a relational being. Any language about the Trinity must keep in mind the importance of relationship. Invoking divine traits cannot suffice to describe the Trinity in their persons.

God the Father

(4) Reference to or address to *God as Father* expresses the intimate relationship that has been revealed in and through Jesus (i.e., the "abba" experience) and is foundational for Jesus' self-understanding and for the Christian faith.[42] This statement requires some further explication.

---

41. Johnson, *She Who Is*, 33–34.

42. For a succinct treatment of this issue as it relates to Christology, see Dermot A. Lane, *Christ at the Centre: Selected Issues in Christology* (Mahwah: Paulist, 1991) 33–46. He utilizes the analysis of Edward Schillebeeckx.

Abba. The Aramaic term *abba,* when discussing patriarchal imagery in the Bible, is at the center of much discussion.[43] This word is found on the lips of Jesus and the early Church (Mark 14:36; Rom 8:15; Gal 4:6). Some maintain that the biblical evidence requires that we always address God as "Father" because Jesus did and taught his disciples to do so (Matt 6:9; Luke 11:2). Others suggest that just because Jesus spoke of God as Father is not reason enough to exclude other titles. Moreover, the Church does not continue to do everything Jesus said or taught in the same way.[44] Again, I do not think the choices are either/or. Let us review some basic data on this topic.

First, on the question of the uniqueness of Jesus' address to God by the use of the Aramaic word, Joseph Fitzmyer, a leading expert on Aramaic, concludes the following: "There is no evidence in the literature of pre-Christian or first-century Palestinian Judaism that '*abbā*' was used in any sense as a personal address for God by an individual—and for Jesus to address God as '*abbā*' or 'Father' is therefore something new."[45] Some evidence of a similar development in late Jewish writings exists, but none of the passages are exactly parallel to the tradition of Jesus. For instance, at Qumran one of the Dead Sea Scrolls contains a prayer that addresses God in Hebrew as "my Father" (4Q372).[46] Also, some Greek Old Testament writings (the Septuagint) contain examples of such prayers (Wis 14:3; Sir 23:1, 4; 3 Macc 5:7; 6:3, 8) and statements viewing God as Father (Wis 2:16; 11:10; Sir 51:10; 3 Macc

43. See most recently Joseph A. Fitzmyer, "ABBĀ and Jesus' Relation to God," in François Refoulé, ed., *À Cause de l'évangile: Mélanges offerts à Dom Jacques Dupont* (Lectio Divina 123; Paris: Cerf, 1985) 15–38. Reprinted in his *According to Paul: Studies in the Theology of the Apostle* (New York/Mahwah: Paulist, 1993) 47–63; James Barr, " 'ABBA' Isn't 'Daddy,' " *JTS* 39 (1988) 28–47; Mary Rose D'Angelo, "*Abba* and 'Father': Imperial Theology and the Jesus Traditions," *JBL* 111 (1992) 611–630, and her "Theology in Mark and Q: Abba and 'Father' in Context," *HTR* 85 (1992) 149–174. I find the comments of Wren (*Language,* 183) about the argumentation of those who want to preserve patriarchal language for God to be overly stereotyped.
44. Johnson, *She Who Is,* 79–80.
45. Fitzmyer, "ABBA," 28. See also, Raymond E. Brown, *The Death of the Messiah* (New York: Doubleday, 1994) 1:172–174.
46. See Eileen M. Schuller, "The Psalm of 4Q372 1 Within the Context of Second Temple Prayer," *CBQ* (1992) 67–79.

2:21; 7:6). Much of the Old Testament data is communal in nature rather than individual. The entire people of Israel view God as their "Father" (Ps 103:13; Tob 13:4; Mal 2:10). Yet one notes the relative sparseness of the term and the fact that nowhere is it employed exactly as in the Aramaic form of Jesus. What about the evidence in the Gospels?

Statistically one can trace an increase in the use of father language in the Gospels. Mark, the oldest Gospel, has four occurrences of the expression "Father" for God, while Luke has fifteen, Matthew has forty-two, and John, the last Gospel to be written, has more than one hundred occurrences. Clearly usage increased in the early decades of Christianity. In even earlier New Testament material we have evidence of the use of this language among Greek-speaking converts (Gal 4:6; Rom 8:15). For St. Paul, calling upon God as "Abba, Father" (both Aramaic and Greek) is a privilege empowered by the Holy Spirit because we are God's own children. Let me summarize seven conclusions that can be made from the biblical evidence.

First, "abba" was remembered and used widely in the Christian tradition (i.e., the diverse communities that preserved the tradition) precisely because it stemmed from Jesus of Nazareth and was a unique aspect of his conscious relationship to God as a son in a fashion that went beyond his Jewish heritage. Second, the early Church preserved the tradition and utilized it in prayer because Jesus desired to share this special relationship with his followers. Third, this heritage was understood by early Christians as, and still remains, foundational to Christian identity (see Eph 3:14-16). Thus it should not be undermined by other forms of address to God. This conclusion does not preclude supplemental addresses to God. Fourth, contrary to popular belief, "abba" does not mean "Daddy," in the sense of a little child's address to his or her father.[47] Rather, it appears to be a respectful and familiar form of address by an adult to a father. Fifth, despite the wishful thinking of some, abba does not seem to represent simply an address to a "parent," as if it embodied the image of mother as well as father. Sixth, despite appearances, the use of abba by Jesus is not a reinforcement of patriarchal tradition. On the contrary, as some feminist scholars have shown, it is radically non-patriarchal,

47. Barr, " 'ABBĀ' Isn't 'Daddy.' "

for it evokes a whole new personal dimension of God that goes beyond the Old Testament tradition and brings the community of disciples into a whole new, intimate relationship to God.[48] Seventh, although the abba experience is an essential aspect of Christian revelation, the relative infrequency of the language in earlier parts of the New Testament materials, and the relative rarity of father language with regard to God in the Old Testament, should give us some pause as to the *frequency* with which we ourselves must invoke it. Excessive use of father language in a context where it can be oppressive seems unwarranted from this data.

At the same time, the biblical perspective is not the only part of the Christian tradition to consider. One of the great aspects about the Catholic faith, as compared to many other Christian denominations, is the respect for the development of the tradition beyond the Bible.[49] The mystical tradition (e.g., Julian of Norwich in the fourteenth century) speaks of God and even addresses God as "Mother."[50] The latter usage of direct address to God as "Mother" goes beyond the testimony of the Bible but is a theological development in the Church's spiritual tradition. Even a modern Pope (John Paul I) has spoken of God as "Mother" in one of his Sunday addresses.[51] Thus, just because the Bible does not address God as mother does not mean that we cannot see in God motherly aspects or describe God as a mother. I will examine this notion further below. For now I want to underscore how moving in this direction must be done with great care so that we do not negate the biblical tradition of Jesus sharing with his disciples his

48. Schneiders, *Women and the Word*, 28–37.

49. This teaching is memorialized in Vatican II by the famous expression of "Scripture" and "sacred Tradition," which represent "the supreme rule" of the Church's faith (*Dei Verbum*, "The Constitution on Divine Revelation," no. 21).

50. See Grace M. Jantzen, *Julian of Norwich: Mystic and Theologian* (New York: Paulist, 1988); Brant Pelphrey, *Christ Our Mother: Julian of Norwich* (The Way of Christian Mystics 7; Wilmington: Michael Glazier, 1989); and V. R. Mollenkott, *Divine Feminine*, and E. Routley, "Gender of God," both listed in the bibliography. For a broad survey of this development see Caroline Walker Bynum, *Jesus as Mother: Studies in the Spirituality of the Middle Ages* (Berkeley: University of California, 1982).

51. September 10, 1978, noted in Hans Dietschy, " 'God is father and mother,' " *Theology Digest* 30 (1982) 132–133.

special relationship to God as "abba," which is Christologically unique and foundational for the life of the Church.

One potential problem with overemphasizing father language is its possible negative psychological impact. Excessive use of father language in the prayers of the current Sacramentary, for example, can be oppressive for a sizeable segment of our congregations. When comparing the English text of the Eucharistic Prayers with the Latin, one notes that numerous times the word "Father" is used for the Latin *Dominus* (Lord). At one time this may have reflected an attempt to make the prayers more familiar and personal, but the effect today on gender sensitive ears is of an unremitting patriarchal use of language.[52] While I suggest we cannot cease to address God as "Father," I also think we need not use that address excessively in liturgy.

Another aspect on the psychological level is that some people (both men and women) may experience father language as difficult because the personal experience of their own fathers may have been abusive, distant, or disdainful. Not everyone can necessarily identify with father language positively, but then the same could be said for mothers. Some have thought to get around the entire problem by invoking the language of the "divine parent" or addressing God as "Father/Mother." But can anyone really think of their own parents, and by analogy God, in such a generic or androgynous way? The concept "parents" of necessity invokes the image of father and mother, but I find it dubious that actually addressing one or the other as "parent" is psychologically appealing.

Essential to remember in this discussion is the *analogical nature of all this language.* I believe that excessive use of father language for God can be properly avoided without detriment to the biblical tradition, yet I would maintain that Christians cannot cease to call out to God as "Abba, Father" without losing something very basic to Christian identity.

God the Son

In discussing the second person of the Trinity, we move to a fifth reason to retain traditional Trinitarian language.

---

52. See Raymond Moloney, *Our Eucharistic Prayers in Worship, Preaching & Study* (Theology and Life 14; Wilmington: Michael Glazier, 1985).

(5) Language referring to *Jesus* takes into account his historical character and his intimate relationship to God as Son of God.
Indeed the doctrine of the incarnation has been tied at times in
the Church's history to the scandalous notion of God taking the
form of human flesh as a man. The very maleness of Jesus seems
at times in history to have been the focus of attention to emphasize this incarnational notion,[53] although the essential scandal of
the incarnation is not tied to the maleness of Jesus but to his humanity.[54]

The designation of Jesus as "Christ" is a more complicated
matter. Although the average Christian would probably use the
names Jesus and Christ interchangeably, from a theological perspective they refer to different aspects of the existence of Jesus
of Nazareth. The name Christ, from the Greek *christos* (a masculine word with a Hebrew background meaning "anointed one"
or "messiah"), is used as a Christological title emphasizing Jesus'
messiahship and his postresurrectional role as Risen Lord and
heavenly intercessor. Some would argue that one could properly
speak of "Christ" as beyond gender identification by virtue of this
exalted state. Certainly the New Testament sometimes speaks of
"putting on" or "clothing oneself" in the Risen Lord Jesus Christ
(Rom 13:14; Gal 3:27; cf. Eph 4:22-24; Col 3:9-10) in a fashion
that transcends gender, for the exhortation applies to all Christians regardless of sex. That Jesus Christ as Risen Lord transcends
human history indicates that there is some *discontinuity* with Jesus
of Nazareth. Thus Jesus Christ, the person, transcends all human
categories, including gender.[55]

Further impetus for referring to Christ in nonmasculine ways
can be derived from the apparent identification the New Testa-

53. See the fascinating study of Leo Steinberg, *The Sexuality of Christ in
Renaissance Art and Modern Oblivion* (New York: Pantheon, 1983), and the
nuancing of Steinberg's position by Caroline Walker Bynum, *Fragmentation
and Redemption: Essays on Gender and the Human Body in Medieval Religion*
(New York: Zone, 1991) 79–117. Also see Mary Podles and Leon J. Podles,
"The Emasculation of God," *America* 161 (November 25, 1989) 372–374.

54. For a succinct discussion of the Incarnation, see Lane, *Christ at the
Centre*, 130–158.

55. See Elizabeth A. Johnson, "The Maleness of Christ," *The Special Nature
of Women?*, Concilium 1991/6, ed. Anne Carr and Elisabeth Schüssler Fiorenza
(Philadelphia: Trinity, 1991) 108–116.

ment makes between Jesus and Lady Wisdom (*sophia*; Matt 11:28-30; 1 Cor 1:24). In the Hebrew tradition Lady Wisdom (*hōkmah*, "the Wisdom Woman") is described as a feminine preexistent power of God who participates in the act of creation and who instructs human beings in the "way of wisdom," the way of living out God's commands in daily life (cf. Prov 1:20-33; 3:13-18; 8:1-36; 9:1-6; Sir 24:1-34; Wis 7:22–9:18; Bar 3:9–4:4). Lady Wisdom is a poetic personification of the important virtue of wisdom that reflects the righteous life in God, and she is sometimes contrasted with another feminine image, the "woman of folly" (Prov 2:16-19; 5:1-6; 7:6-27; 9:13-18).

To invoke Christ as *sophia*, the embodied wisdom of God described in feminine terms, is certainly a sound biblical tradition (Bishops' Guidelines #28), and its influence on Christology has been profound (e.g., John's Gospel). But what role should this tradition play in the pertinent question of inclusive language? The feminine traditions are still dominated from a biblical perspective by the masculine imagery, but the feminine notion of Sophia can provide some much needed counterbalance. At the same time, a caution with regard to this language is in order. The personification of Wisdom in the Old Testament tradition is not entirely personal in nature, for it sometimes represents a power or an aspect of God present in the act of creation. The Risen Christ, however, must be viewed as a person and cannot be reduced to being an "aspect" of God. Whereas some feminist scholars might suggest that this image *supplant* the traditional male images used for Christ in order to overcome centuries of misogyny, I suggest along with other scholars that it should be used to *supplement* them.

In the same way the New Testament shows other modes of viewing Jesus Christ beyond the masculine dimensions of humanity. Thus John's Gospel most notably refers to Jesus through a vast array of images. Jesus is the "word made flesh" (1:14), the "lamb of God" (1:29, 36; cf. 19:36; Rev 5:6; 14:1; 21:23), the "bread of life" (6:35), the "light of the world" (8:12; cf. 1:1-8), "the way, the truth, and the life" (14:6), the "resurrection and the life" (11:25), "the true vine" (15:1), and so on. Precedent exists in the New Testament, therefore, for going beyond the masculine dimensions of Jesus' existence when speaking of his exalted state as Lord of heaven and earth. We should also note, however, that such imagery is still tied intimately to the person of Jesus, a dimension that should not be lost in an attempt to be inclusive.

A more important reason for not replacing male imagery in relation to Christ with alternatives is from a doctrinal angle. Despite the biblical testimony of some discontinuity with Jesus of Nazareth, as we saw above, there is also a biblical tradition of *continuity*. At the heart of the New Testament teaching about the faith in Jesus Christ is both the *bodily* resurrection and the continuity between the Risen Christ and Jesus of Nazareth. For instance, Mark's Gospel explicitly connects the "Jesus of Nazareth, who was crucified," with the Risen Christ (Mark 16:6; Matt 28:5-6; cf. Acts 1:11). Thus I find artistic attempts to represent Christ as a woman questionable for a setting in public worship. Take, for example, Edwina Sandys' controversial sculpture *Christa*, which was hung in the Cathedral of St. John the Divine in New York City in 1984. It portrays a naked woman with arms outstretched in cruciform fashion. Without any evaluation of it as an art form, one can ask if it is an appropriate symbol of ecclesial faith suitable for Christian *public* prayer. What may work to evoke various alternative reflections in the private sphere can too easily mislead people in a public sphere. The identification between the crucified Jesus of Nazareth and the Risen Lord is essential in the Christian tradition, even though the Risen Christ transcends all human categories. Although some of the resurrection texts indicate that Jesus had been so transformed by the resurrection as to be unrecognizable at first glance (Luke 24:16, 31; John 20:14-16), nonetheless the essential identification between Jesus and the Risen Christ in *bodily* fashion is essential (John 21:7, 12; even to the point of apologetic motifs, such as the eating of the fish in Luke 24:42-43).

I am reminded of the great scene of Paul's conversion as it is portrayed in Acts 9. Paul falls to the ground at the flash of a heavenly light, and a voice speaks, "Saul, Saul, why do you persecute me?" Paul responds, "Who are you, *Lord*?" And the voice replies, "I am *Jesus*, whom you are persecuting" (Acts 9:4-5; cf. 22:7-8; 26:14-15). The identification between Jesus of Nazareth and the Risen Christ is preserved even in the story of the one who would consider himself no less an apostle because he was called by the latter rather than the former (1 Cor 15:9-10; 2 Cor 11:5).

Another example of the Risen Christ in the traditional role of a male is the image of the bridegroom, an image that also appears in Jesus' own teaching as recorded in the Synoptic Gospels (Mark 2:19-20; Matt 9:15; Luke 5:34-35). Christ is the bridegroom and the Church is the bride, as is found in the comparison between the human marriage relationship and the Christ-Church relationship in Ephesians 5:22-32 (cf. 2 Cor 11:2; John 3:29) or the symbolic woman in Revelation 12.[56] The Old Testament exhibits such imagery as well, symbolic of the relationship between God as the husband and the people of Israel as wife. For example, Isaiah employs the analogy:

> For as a young man marries a young woman,
>   so shall your builder marry you,
> and as the bridegroom rejoices over the bride,
>   so shall your God rejoice over you (Isa 62:5).

An excerpt from the poignant description in the prophet Hosea (Hos 2:1-20) provides an even more striking example.

> On that day, says the LORD, you will call me, "My husband," and no longer will you call me, "My Baal." And I will take you for my wife forever; I will take you for my wife in righteousness and in justice, in steadfast love, and in mercy. I will take you for my wife in faithfulness; and you shall know the LORD (Hos 2:16, 19-20; cf. the Song of Songs).

The results of this discussion of God the Son indicate that because the Risen Christ now exists beyond time, space, and history as Risen Lord means that he transcends history, but not that he is suddenly sexless. While the cosmic Christ supersedes and transcends humanity, he does not reject it. Some scholars fear that "to make of the maleness of Jesus Christ a christological principle is to deny the universality of salvation."[57] To use the maleness of Jesus Christ to oppress women would indeed be wrong, for all who wish to follow Jesus Christ, women and men alike, are called

---

56. The Bishops' Guidelines note that normally the Church is to be referred to in *neuter* third person singular except in instances, such as here, where a feminine image would require feminine pronouns (no. 31).

57. Johnson, *She Who Is*, 73.

to full discipleship. His transformed humanity represents salvation and redemption for all humanity. In this sense, his humanity rather than his maleness is the primary category of incarnation, but one cannot forego his human identity. My conclusion is that we need to retain a balance. Perhaps the Creed can be our model. Just as in the Creed the incarnational tension between Jesus as fully God and fully human must be maintained, so in the notion of the Jesus of history and the Christ of faith a tension between continuity and discontinuity must be maintained.

God the Spirit

When discussing the third person of the Trinity, we encounter the sixth and seventh reasons to retain traditional Trinitarian language.

(6) Language referring to the *Spirit* is perhaps even more complicated on the question of gender. Although a few have seen in the Spirit the feminine dimension of God, this notion goes beyond the biblical testimony. Elizabeth Johnson, whom I have quoted before, points out the precariousness of making the Holy Spirit *the* feminine dimension of God.[58] In the Christian tradition the Holy Spirit has been essentially faceless or amorphous even though the Spirit is clearly identified as the third person of the Blessed Trinity.

Neither the Greek (*pneuma*, neuter; *parakletos*, masculine) nor the Hebrew (*ruach*, feminine or masculine) can be construed to be exclusively feminine (Latin = *spiritus*, masculine). More importantly, the terms "masculine" and "feminine," when referring to the morphology of words, are grammatical categories unrelated to the question of physical gender. For example, the designation of the Spirit as Paraclete in John's Gospel (John 14:15-16, 26; 15:26; 16:7-11), connotes one who is a comforter, advocate, or counselor, images that go beyond masculine dimensions. Some scholars also propose using a Jewish concept of Shekinah (one who dwells, indwelling) found in later rabbinic materials as a way of speaking of God's presence in a non-gender manner and an image for Spirit, but this does not have great appeal from a Christian perspective.[59]

58. Ibid., 50.
59. See ibid., 85–86. For the potential of this concept in Jewish-Christian

Traditionally, Christian art has often portrayed the Spirit as a dove, representing an ethereal and graceful being, able to fly here and there effortlessly and with beauty of motion. Such imagery is rooted in the Bible's own portrayal of the spirit of God as a bird. In the creation story God's spirit (Hebrew = spirit, wind) is said to hover or sweep over the waters of the earth (Gen 1:2), and the same verb is used to describe the action of an eagle hovering over its young in the nest (Deut 32:11).[60] In the Gospels the spirit is described at the baptism of Jesus *like* a dove (Mark 1:10; Matt 3:16; Luke 3:22; John 1:32).

Elsewhere God (not the Spirit) is also directly compared to an eagle whose protective wings spread over a people in difficult times (Isa 31:5; cf. Exod 19:4; Deut 32:11-12), and the people often cry out to God in need of "the shadow of your wings" (Pss 17:8; 36:7; 57:1; 91:1, 4). A feminist theologian recently shared with me her experience of being in the Southern Hemisphere (New Zealand) and witnessing the flight of the huge albatrosses. Though we in the Northern Hemisphere know these birds only in caricature, she insisted that the beauty of their flight, despite their awkward eleven-foot wingspan, suddenly made her reconsider imagery for the Holy Spirit. Although she had often referred to the Holy Spirit as "she," she now indicated (with just a hint of humor) that the image of a bird to symbolize this aspect of the Godhead may not be so bad after all!

(7) Another important aspect of changing Trinitarian language is the possible serious consequence with regard to sacramental validity. Some may be tempted to use an alternate formula as a substitute for the traditional Trinitarian one. But canon law (Canon 849) explicitly requires the use of a precise Trinitarian formulation if baptism is to be not only licit but also valid.[61] Using a substitute

---

dialogue, see Michael E. Lodahl, *Shekinah/Spirit: Divine Presence in Jewish and Christian Religion* (New York: Paulist, 1992).

60. Notice that the NRSV translates Deut 32:11-12 using the neuter "its wings." Some insist that the eagle portrayed here is a mother eagle caring for her young, but the text is ambiguous on that score. A father eagle could be just as protective of its young.

61. See John M. Huels, "Canon 849: Defect of Form in Baptism," *Roman Replies and CLSA Advisory Opinions* (Washington, D.C.: Canon Law Society of America, 1990) 91-92, and James C. Gurzynski, "Canons 850 and 1117:

or an incomplete formula jeopardizes the individual receiving the sacrament.

With these seven reasons offered as rationale for preserving traditional use of Trinitarian language at this time, we can see some of the complexity and tensions within the biblical and theological traditions of the Church. Much is at stake when we consider linguistic changes in these categories. Of utmost importance in dealing with language for the Trinitarian God is the care we must take to avoid "neutering" God or "depersonalizing" God in the interests of non-offensive language. At the core of the Judeo-Christian tradition is the revelation of God in terms of personhood and relationship. God cannot simply be viewed in terms of a primal force or a collection of characteristic traits (Exod 3:6, 14; Mark 12:26). Personhood and relationality are two essential aspects of the doctrine of the Trinity. Although God remains mysterious and incomprehensible in essence, nonetheless Christian tradition holds that God is revealed to us as a *communion* of Father, Son, and Holy Spirit. This elusive God chooses to be revealed in ways that reflect personal identity and relationship. This observation warns us against too facile a solution to the problem of exclusive language with reference to God.

In the end one can see some of the difficulties biblical translators face with regard to imaging both persons and God. There are no absolute guidelines that can be applied in each and every case. Decisions about language must be made on a passage-to-passage basis, keeping in mind the difficulties that may be encountered and keeping in check the urge simply to change every perceived exclusive word. Ramifications of language must be carefully examined and theological issues ferreted out. Since this is the situation on a professional scholarly level, how much more caution is needed on the parochial level where false impressions are easily conveyed!

How Variations in the Baptismal Formula Impact the Validity of Marriage," *Roman Replies and CLSA Advisory Opinions* (Washington, D.C.: Canon Law Society of America, 1992) 101–104. I am grateful to Randolph R. Calvo for providing these specific references.

Chapter III.

Practical Guidelines for Inclusive Language in Liturgy

As stated in the introduction, a primary goal of this book is to provide a practical guide for those involved in planning and executing parish liturgies. This chapter fleshes out the general guidelines as they apply to specific situations. In many ways the advice given here is common sense. But my experience of many parochial situations has been that the topic of inclusive language is often so emotionally charged that common sense gets overshadowed by gut reactions. The purpose of this chapter is to provide a basic set of guidelines that respect the liturgical rubrics and yet lay out a way to be as inclusive as one possibly can within the current limitations.

1. Prepare in advance. The overarching principle is: always prepare in advance! No procedure is more hazardous than changing texts in midstream without having prepared them ahead of time. Liturgy planners, readers, musicians, preachers, and presiders have the responsibility to work together to coordinate all facets of the liturgical celebration. They should always prepare all the texts (liturgical and biblical) in advance and note any foreseeable difficulties with exclusive language. Given the fact that the *NABRNT*, which is sensitive to inclusive language issues, has been approved by the bishops for use in Catholic worship, there is no excuse for lack of advance preparation even with regard to the biblical readings.

2. Beware of changing words. Making word changes can be quite risky. In order to illustrate this principle, I will discuss three primary areas of concern: communal prayers, the creed, and hymns.

a) Communal Prayers. Since the very nature of liturgy is communal, it is essential to see the liturgy as an act that joins the local Church with the whole universal Church at prayer. Liturgy is a public act that involves and affects many other people. One should therefore be most cautious about changing the words of *communal* prayers. It is not within an individual's jurisdiction to change the official texts of the Eucharistic liturgy, especially the Eucharistic Prayers and those Eucharistic texts that are prayed by the community in common, for example, before the prayer over the gifts.

In practice, many individuals have taken to changing a few small words in two specific locations. The first is in the dialogue to the Preface of the Eucharistic Prayer. When the presider says, "Let us give thanks to the Lord our God," the congregation's response is, "It is right to give *him* [God] thanks and praise." Another instance is in the community's prayer at the preparation of the gifts. In response to the presider's invitation, the congregation says, "May the Lord accept this sacrifice at your hands for the praise and glory of his [God's] name, for our good, and the good of all his [the or God's] Church." One can surmise that these minor changes (noted in brackets) may well go the way of dropping "men" from "for all men" in the institution narrative. Common parochial practice may influence later official liturgical practice.

A major problem with the practice of changing such words in my judgment arises when individuals in a congregation begin what amounts to a shouting match to see who can say the offensive or alternative word the loudest. The purpose is to make a theological point rather than to pray. Some worry that this produces cacophony and disrupts the unified prayer. More important to my mind is that it makes of the Eucharist a political battleground. It works against the real unity of the Body of Christ we celebrate every time we gather to "remember the Lord until he comes in glory." While I hope this problem will be resolved in a future edition of the Sacramentary, my advice is to avoid a theological tennis match at liturgy over relatively insignificant matters.

b) The Creed. The creed provides another delicate area where exclusive language unnecessarily intrudes.[62] The linguistic evidence is clear that the intention of the creed is to be inclusive rather than exclusive. Where the English text of the Nicene Creed reads "for us *men* and for our salvation" the Latin uses the word *homines* (human beings) rather than the more restrictive *vir* for male human beings. This mistranslation also occurs in the section on the incarnation. The English translation has "and became man" but the Latin text reads, *"homo factus est,"* emphasizing Jesus' humanity, not his maleness. In fact, the New Testament text that undergirds the creed in this section is John 1:14, the famous text, "And the Word became flesh. . . ." This Greek text also employs a more general term *(sarx)*, which emphasizes Jesus' humanity rather than his maleness.

Although it is not inaccurate to say Jesus became "man" rather than "human," if this language is perceived to perpetuate an exclusivity, I believe it is better to change it. We have seen above that Jesus Christ transcends human categories and incarnationally is the paradigm of salvation for all, male and female. Clearly the care with which the Creed was formulated centuries ago by using a general expression for humanity rather than an androcentric one should give us a clue as to how to understand the mystery of the incarnation. The difficulty with this section of the Mass is, of course, that everyone recites it together. While it is easy and non-obtrusive simply to drop the word "men" in the first instance, the second one ("and became man") yields too many alternatives to be effective. This is one text where we will probably have to await a new translation of the Sacramentary to produce an efficacious change that more clearly reflects the meaning of the Creed itself. The NCCB considered a new translation of the Creed in June 1995, and slight changes were approved.

c) Hymns. Concern for inclusivity in both society and in the Church has had an impact on the composition and publication

62. For some practical suggestions on the Creed in Sunday worship, see Ronald D. Witherup, "Can We Save the Creed?" *The Priest* 48:6 (1992) 14–18.

of hymns for liturgy. Most composers and music publishers are sensitive to the issue of inclusive language, and consequently publish music that reflects this perspective. Many parishes have also become sensitized to this issue and desire to use inclusive music. Unfortunately, economic and sometimes sentimental reasons force many parishes to use older hymnals that do not contain inclusive language. What basic guidelines can be applied to this situation?

Several guidelines apply to amending hymns:

(1) In the amending and reproduction of hymns copyright laws should always be respected. Although many older hymns are in the public domain, churches have a moral and legal obligation to respect the rights of those who hold the copyright to hymns. Before any changes can be made in copyrighted hymns, explicit permission of the copyright owner is required.

(2) Amend texts carefully if such can be done without serious damage to either the sense or rhythm (meter, etc.) of the hymn and without violating copyright laws. Often simple word changes will suffice to make a text inclusive (e.g., "man" or "men" to "all," "we," or "us"). Although one is tempted to replace "he" with the one-syllable word "God" in order to avoid an exclusive term, this interchange does not always work smoothly for purposes of singing. Some one-syllable words are naturally longer in pronunciation than others.

(3) As in the case of the spoken word, linguistic changes in hymns should be prepared in advance. If possible, changes should appear in the copies available to the congregation. Asking a congregation to change a word or two spontaneously while they sing a hymn may seem fairly simple, but confusion can easily arise when they are asked to make numerous changes of words or expressions. This practice unfortunately discourages active participation and encourages resistance to inclusive language.

(4) Leave out verses of hymns that may be exclusive in language only if this can be done without damaging the sense of the text. It may also be possible to alternate stanzas with feminine and masculine imagery in some hymns, for example, "God of Our Fathers" with "God of Our Mothers."

(5) If the hymn is virtually a biblical reading set to music the same guidelines as those for biblical texts above (chapter two) should be observed.

(6) Do not use hymns that are not able to be properly amended.

(7) The original Grail translation of the Psalms, often used because of its beautiful musical settings, is unfortunately laden with exclusive language and, perhaps more seriously, does not divide many of the psalms into sense-patterns that accord with parallelism in the psalms. A new translation (G.I.A. Pub., 1993) is now available. A new study version of psalms has been prepared and has received approbation from the NCCB (*The Psalter* [Chicago: Liturgy Training Publications, 1994]). Other editions of the psalms are available for use, and many newer hymnals contain musical settings of the psalms that employ inclusive language.

3. **Include that which is truly inclusive.** Many times I have been struck by an incongruity in the Eucharistic liturgy concerning the use and misuse of inclusive language. The ease with which readers and presiders seemingly feel free to change the biblical texts (often with a distinct lack of knowledge of the underlying original language) and yet blithely proceed to repeat exclusive terms in contexts that could readily and rubrically be changed has baffled me! Within the rubrics set forth in the Sacramentary (Chap. II; Art. 10–13), the principal celebrant or president of the assembly is given considerable freedom to adapt the admonitions, greetings, "instructions and words of introduction and conclusion" so that inclusive language may be used. In addition, the tropes of the Penitential Rite and the petitions of the Prayer of the Faithful are freely adaptable and should always employ inclusive language.

One should note the rubric from *The Order of Mass* concerning the Penitential Rite, the invitation to the prayer over the gifts (the "Orate Fratres"), and other admonitions or invitations:

> At the discretion of the priest, other words which seem more suitable under the circumstances, such as, "friends," "dearly beloved," etc., may be used. This also applies to parallel instances in the liturgy.[63]

All other liturgical actions and texts, such as homilies, extra-biblical readings or meditations, petitions, announcements, etc.,

---

63. See also Chapter II, Articles 10–13 in the "General Instruction on the Roman Missal" for the role of the presider in adapting prayers in the Eucharist. M. A. Simcoe, *The Liturgy Documents: A Parish Resource* (Chicago: Liturgy Training Publications, 1985) 52–53.

should always employ inclusive language. These parts of the Eucharist could also provide occasions to use more balanced biblical imagery (e.g., Sophia—"divine Wisdom"; or God as a nurturing mother as in Isa 46:3-4) or to call attention to the mysterious, incomprehensible nature of God.

The language addressing and referring to the worshiping community (e.g., "sons," "brothers," "brethren," etc.) should always be inclusive (e.g., "sisters and brothers," "friends in Christ," etc.; as in the Bishops' Guidelines #17).

The language referring to God in the Judeo-Christian tradition is predominantly but not exclusively masculine in character. Although this fact remains problematic, as we have seen above, and is the subject of intense study by ICEL, the U.S. Bishops' Committee on Liturgy, and the revisers of the Lectionary and Sacramentary, it seems premature to adopt definitive alternatives. We simply have to "live with" present limitations of language.

4. Respect the order of importance of texts. An order of importance exists concerning concrete situations in liturgy when the question of substitutions or alternatives arises. Not all liturgical texts are of equal weight. Thus some are more easily subject to editing than others. The elements in liturgy least susceptible to linguistic change under present rubrics are the readings from Sacred Scripture and direct quotations of Scripture (e.g., the Lord's Prayer), yet the new, more inclusive approved translations, as we have mentioned above, now obviate some difficulties. It is far easier to change prayers or readings spoken by an individual than it is to change parts of the liturgy spoken by the entire assembly. The reality of the present situation has inherent limitations. There are no absolutes in how to remain sensitive to inclusive language issues and yet remain true to the liturgical traditions of the Church. Nevertheless, within these limitations, every worshiping community needs to work toward greater sensitivity and responsibility in the use of liturgical language.

5. Be inconspicuous when substituting. Another important principle is that substitutions should be as inconspicuous as possible, taking into account the structure, rhythm, cadence, and sense of the passage. Substitutions should be subtle enough that they seem natural and express a message in a way that does not draw attention only to themselves. The psalms offer a special case for concern because of their considerable exclusive language. Where possible within the guidelines for Scripture above, inclusive language should be used. For example, "Happy the man who" changed to "Happy the one who" or "Happy those who" may actually render a more accurate translation of the Psalm's intention. Fortunately, the revised *Psalms of the New American Bible* are to be incorporated into the new Lectionary and will resolve many current problems.

6. Always follow the rules of English grammar. At all times in making changes in the language of a given text, care should be taken to follow the rules of proper English grammar. Grammarians, however, do not always agree about such rules. Thus, the *Oxford English Dictionary* recognizes that "they" is often used in reference to a singular noun made universal by "every," "any," "no," etc., or is applied to one of either sex (i.e., "he" or "she"). The usage of the plural for the indefinite singular pronoun is also recognized by the National Council of Teachers of English.[64] Other grammarians oppose this usage. The choice appears to be a matter of personal taste. In any case, proper English grammar should be used and, if necessary, an authoritative English grammar or dictionary should be consulted for guidelines.[65]

7. Consult with experts. This brief handbook cannot address all circumstances that are likely to arise about such a complex issue as inclusive language in liturgy. When there is uncertainty about what course of action to take in changing the language of a biblical text, changing a difficult liturgical text, or utilizing an alternative translation, my advice is to consult with someone with more expertise, for example, an official from the diocesan liturgical commission.

64. "Guidelines for Nonsexist Use of Language in NCTE Publications (Revised, 1985)" (Urbana, Ill.: National Council of Teachers of English) 3.

65. For example, H. W. Fowler, *A Dictionary of Modern English Usage,* 2d ed. (Oxford: Clarendon, 1965).

Chapter IV.

Ongoing Developments

After this book was substantially written, a controversy erupted on the use of inclusive language in Catholic worship that illustrates the ongoing tension surrounding this issue. The purpose of this chapter is to review some of this recent history. I will not repeat my earlier discussion, but will illustrate the issues with specific biblical examples.

A. Brief History of the Controversy

The following synopsis summarizes recent developments over the use of inclusive language in Catholic worship. Two factors apparently provide the background for the sequence of events described below. One was the Vatican decision not to use inclusive language in the newly published catechism. That decision may have set the tone for the review of recent biblical translations for liturgical use. The other was the long delay in approval of the proposed new American lectionary using the revised translations of the *New American Bible* (including the revised edition of the Psalms).[66] Nonetheless, the focus of the controversy was on the *NRSV* edition of the Bible.

66. I am grateful to Jerry Filteau of the Catholic News Service for providing me news source material.

On October 25, 1994, the secretary of the Congregation for Divine Worship and the Sacraments, Archbishop Geraldo Agnelo, announced during an interview that permission to use the *NRSV* for public worship had been rescinded by the Congregation for the Doctrine of the Faith. Earlier permission for its use had been granted by the Worship Congregation in 1992. The decision to rescind permission affected both the NCCB and its Canadian counterpart, the CCCB, which already had been using a lectionary with the *NRSV* translation since 1992. No specific reasons for the withdrawal of permission were given, although news accounts indicated that the matters of inclusive language were of a doctrinal nature and not merely stylistic.

On October 26, 1994, in a phone interview for Catholic News Service, Bishop Donald W. Trautman, a biblical scholar and chair of the U.S. Bishops' Committee on Liturgy, defended the use of inclusive language as "a necessity in our American idiom and culture today." He indicated that inclusive language was necessary in Scripture, liturgy, and catechetics, and he expressed hope that the decision would lead to further dialogue between U.S. Scripture scholars and officials from the doctrinal congregation.[67]

On November 1, 1994, the president of the NCCB, Archbishop (later Cardinal) William Keeler indicated that the decision apparently had been made in a July 27, 1994, letter to him by the Worship Congregation, which had been interpreted not as a formal decree but as part of the ongoing discussions over the proposed American lectionary. He also emphasized that the rescinded permission applied only to public worship. The *NRSV* was still acceptable for private study and prayer.

In mid-November 1994 the Canadian bishops received permission to continue to use their *NRSV* lectionary on an interim basis until further discussions could be held.

In mid-January 1995 a delegation of bishops and Scripture scholars from the U.S. went to Rome for a consultation on these matters. The group was chaired by Bishop Trautman and included Bishop Richard J. Sklba, chair of the Bishops' Committee for the

---

67. Jerry Filteau, "Bishop Trautman Calls for Inclusive Language in Liturgy," Catholic News Service (October 26, 1994).

Review of Scripture Translations, Franciscan Father Alexander A. Di Lella, Scripture Professor at The Catholic University of America (Washington, D.C.), and Jesuit Father Richard J. Clifford, Professor of Old Testament at the Weston Jesuit School of Theology (Cambridge, Massachusetts). The Vatican delegation was not announced. Bishop Trautman described the outcome of the consultation as "definitely productive," but details were not released.[68]

This brief scenario indicates just how sensitive an issue inclusive language continues to be. A look at some of the disputed issues will provide a helpful overview of some complications in the recent discussions about inclusive language.

B. Disputed Issues

What are the issues the Vatican has raised concerning the *NRSV* translation? No formal decree has spelled out publicly the specific issues at stake, but news accounts indicated that the concerns were "doctrinal" and not merely a matter of style. One unnamed official quoted in the original news story pointed out two problems with the *NRSV* translation.[69] The first was that using a dual expression such as "men and women" instead of "man" tended to "divide" human persons into two categories, while using a generic word like "humanity" was considered overly abstract. A second concern was that avoiding the male pronoun in some instances blurs the Christological meanings of texts.

Before examining these and other issues, two comments warrant repetition in this context: *no translation of the Bible is perfect,* and *every translation is an interpretation.* Thus, as I have indicated in some examples in previous chapters, every biblical translation has some limitations. The *NRSV* is no exception. The goal is not to make a translation simply literal, but also to make it both accurate and sensible to the contemporary audience. An added comment is to note that this latest controversy centers on

68. John Thavis, "Inclusive Language Meeting Called 'Definitively Productive,' " Catholic News Service (January 21, 1995).

69. John Thavis, "Vatican Rejects NRSV Bible For Liturgical, Catechetical Use," Catholic News Service (October 25, 1994).

the use of inclusive language for human beings (that is, the horizontal references). The *NRSV* translation (as do the revisions of the *New American Bible*) retains the traditional language with reference to God (vertical references).

1. Designations for Human Beings

The objection against the use of generic words for the human being seems arbitrary or betrays a lack of knowledge about contemporary American English usage. I discussed in chapter two the principles regarding reference to human beings in biblical texts. I also indicated that English is a living language that continues to change with common usage. Whereas it was perfectly acceptable at one time in the history of English to refer to human beings as "mankind," that is no longer acceptable common English usage. In contemporary English "man" no longer connotes both men and women; rather, it is seen as a gender-specific term.[70] This is not merely an academic concern. Nor is it merely a "modern" phenomenon. Since the nineteenth century (and even earlier in the period of "Middle English," ca. 1300–1500 A.D.) grammarians have recognized that the word "man" had lost its original generic meaning.[71] Standard publishing houses today have adopted rules requiring use of inclusive language. If one wants to emphasize the unity of both genders, terms like "human beings," "human persons," "people," "humanity," "humankind," and the like should be sufficient to translate accurately those passages that refer to humans in a generic way.

To object that "humanity" is too abstract seems more a matter of style than substance. Certainly, some contemporary expressions are less elegant and perhaps more cumbersome to use in some instances (such as "humankind"). On the other hand, when such expressions translate the proper underlying biblical words that refer to human beings generically, then they are more accurate than previous, gender-specific English terms.

---

70. The complications and history of this change are examined in Dennis Baron's excellent book, *Grammar and Gender* (chapter 8, pp. 137–161), listed in the bibliography.

71. Baron, *Grammar and Gender*, 137–141.

The most prominent example of this issue, which we noted only briefly in chapter two, is Genesis 1:26-27. This text speaks of the creation of the human being (Hebrew *adam*) both male and female. Both the Septuagint *(anthrōpos)* and the Latin Vulgate *(hominem)* use generic human terms. Whereas the *RSV* used the word "man," the *NRSV* uses the word "humankind." The *REB* has the expression "human beings." In any case, accurate translation requires a gender-inclusive expression for the underlying biblical text (also in Gen 9:6 and other places). In line with contemporary English usage the word "man" no longer communicates this generic sense for most people.

We could examine many other examples, but the main point would remain the same. In the case of horizontal inclusive language, doctrinal concerns are more illusory than real regarding the use of acceptable modern English to communicate faithfully the sense of the biblical text. Objections to the *NRSV* on these grounds are ill-founded.

2. *Christological Concerns*[72]

A second concern focused on Christological meanings of texts. These issues most likely center around the so-called "messianic psalms" and texts that use the expression "Son of Man." We already dealt with some issues in chapter two, but we will examine a few more explicit examples here.

One objection has been raised in public about the inclusive translation of some of the psalms not just in the *NRSV* but also in the *NJB* and the *Psalms* (revised *NAB*). Jesuit Father Joseph Fessio has objected to the translation of Psalm 1:1 as "Happy are *those* who do not follow the advice of the wicked" (*NRSV*). He believes the use of the plural "those" obscures the Christological meaning of this text.[73] Since the text literally reads, "Blessed is the *man* [Hebrew *'ish*] who . . .," he believes that the inclusive translation does not allow for the Christological interpretation that this "man" represents Christ and does not apply merely to every human being. He bolsters his claim by asserting that the Christo-

---

72. For this section I refer the reader to the excellent summary of these issues by Joseph Jensen, *America* 171:14 (November 5, 1994) 14–18.
73. *Catholic World Report* 4:2 (1994) 64.

logical interpretation was taught by all the Church fathers and "unbroken Tradition." The real crux of Fr. Fessio's objections, however, center on the accusation that such inclusive language translations deprive people of the "Christ of the Psalms," and that this action is ironically promoted by the American bishops themselves by means of their approval of the revised *Psalms* of the *NAB*. His objections, however, have been rightly countered by a Jesuit biblical scholar, Richard J. Clifford.[74] Clifford points out that the Christological interpretation of Psalm 1 was a minority position of the Church Fathers. He quotes St. Jerome as an example: "such an interpretation certainly shows a lack of experience and knowledge, for if that happy man is Christ, and Christ gave the law, how can the words: 'But delights in the law of the Lord' apply to Christ?" An added point would be that here as in other places in the Hebrew Bible the word *'ish* does not mean "man" (= male) as is normally the case. Rather it stands for the universal human being, regardless of gender, who is called to observe God's law. Thus, the most appropriate translation in such instances still favors an inclusive expression. In essence, the charge that the use of horizontal inclusive language obscures the Christological meaning of the psalms is, in such cases, exaggerated.

Psalm 8 is another prominent text that attracts some controversy. The pertinent part of this poetic text reads:

> When I look at your heavens, the work of your fingers,
>   the moon and the stars that you have established;
> what are *human beings* that you are mindful of them,
>   *mortals* that you care for them? (vv. 3–4).

This *NRSV* translation of the italicized words properly gives the original sense of the Hebrew psalm. The psalm uses a poetic expression for "human beings" (*enosh* = literally, man) and a Hebrew idiom for a "mortal" (*ben adam* = literally, son of man). This latter expression is the common Hebrew way of speaking about humans in a collective sense, that is, individuals who belong to the group, "human beings." Consequently, the psalmist compares human existence to that of the universe and is in awe that God has chosen to make human beings so exalted in creation.

74. *National Jesuit News* 23:6 (April/May 1994). I am grateful to Fr. Clifford for this reference. See also his article, "The Bishops, the Bible and Liturgical Language," *America* 172:19 (May 27, 1995) 12–16.

The difficulty with such an inclusive translation arises because of the treatment Psalm 8:3-4 receives in the New Testament (Heb 2:6). The author of Hebrews quotes the psalm (albeit from the Greek Septuagint rather than the Hebrew Bible) in the context of speaking of the exaltation of Jesus. The author makes a clear connection between the common Hebrew expression "son of man" and the Gospel Christological title, "son of man," which Jesus is shown using as a self-designation. In this case, in my judgment, the *NRSV*'s use of the expressions "human beings" and "mortals" *in Hebrews* obscures the Christological connection that the Letter to the Hebrews makes. This judgment would also accord with the bishops' guidelines (#29) where instances of Christological interpretation are to be respected. But this does not necessarily mean that the original sense of the Hebrew psalm itself was therefore Christological. One notes that the revised *New American Bible* retains the traditional language of "man" and "son of man" for Hebrews 2:6 even though the revised translation of Psalm 8:3-4 properly uses "humans" and "mortals." In fact, the use of the psalm by the author of Hebrews is essentially an application of the psalm's words in a very different sense than the psalm itself communicates. Thus, even if the *NRSV*'s translation in Hebrews can be viewed as flawed, it would not negate the same translation in the psalm itself.

A third prominent passage is Daniel 7:13 that has also received much attention from scholars. The Book of Daniel recounts one of the prophet's visions thus:

> As I watched in the night visions,
>   I saw one like a *human being*
>   coming with the clouds of heaven.
> And he came to the Ancient One
>   and was presented before him.

Again, the expression "human being" is literally "son of man" (Aramaic *bar enosh*), which is acknowledged in the footnote of the *NRSV*. This passage also receives much attention in the New Testament because the expression became part of the Christological tradition of titles for Jesus Christ. Scholars variously interpret the original passage in Daniel as representing an angel or a collective group, such as the people of Israel, but the New Testament associates the figure with Jesus (Matt 8:20; 24:30; 26:64; Rev 14:14). Here again the *NRSV* does somewhat obscure the later Christian understanding of the passage, yet the later interpretation is taken up only in the context of the New Testament. The original sense of Daniel is to communicate that the figure looks like a human being (son of man). It is appropriate that the Old Testament, even as a Christian book, is allowed to speak in its own context. The inclusive translation "human being" is thus not inappropriate, especially when footnotes in the Bible provide the literal sense.

C. A Pastoral Example

Thus far we have been examining what might appear to be merely complicated academic issues that really have little pastoral ramification. I have insisted throughout this book that inclusive language issues have pastoral ramifications, and that they also are more complicated than we would like them to be. That is why I favor a cautious approach to inclusive language. In my judgment, it would be better if sensible inclusive language decisions were left to experts and officially promoted by the Church rather than ignored, opposed, or denied altogether. In my judgment, the inclusive language guidelines of the American bishops, which we have referenced throughout this book, have been admirable in promoting sensible, justifiable translations of the Bible for public consumption. Most of the objections to inclusive language on principle are based upon needless fear and incomplete knowledge. To jeopardize the progress in inclusive language that these guidelines have promoted will only lead to further confusion in the pews. I would like to illustrate this point by recounting a recent incident I experienced at a reconciliation service.

The presider had chosen as the text for a general reconciliation service the story of the woman caught in adultery (John 8:1-11). He also wanted to be sensitive to his congregation. He decided to use an inclusive language translation (the *NRSV*, at the time permitted). However, he found the text too exclusive. Why concentrate only on women? Don't men commit adultery, too? Thus, for the service he changed the details of the story. The text became "the people caught in adultery"! He changed all the references throughout the reading to the plural and thus made it "inclusive."

At first glance the change may seem to some harmless enough. Both men and women do engage in adultery. Making the text more "inclusive" seemingly applies the message of both the sin and the forgiveness of Jesus in a more equitable way. However, these changes unfortunately alter the historical realities of the text and ultimately sanitize the message of the text.

The historical reality of the laws of adultery in the time of Jesus required the death of a *woman* (but not the man!) caught in adultery (Lev 20:10; Deut 22:22). This is an essential part of the story in John's Gospel.

> The scribes and the Pharisees brought a woman who had been caught in adultery; and making her stand before all of them, they said to him, "Teacher, this woman was caught in the very act of committing adultery. Now in the law Moses commanded us to stone such women. Now what do you say?" They said this to test him, so that they might have some charge to bring against him (John 8:3-6).

The purpose of the incident is to trap Jesus by making him act against the law. Thus, when Jesus pronounces his unwillingness to condemn the woman (v. 11), he not only brings her the gift of reconciliation, but he also turns upside down the requirements of the Torah in its stipulations regarding adultery. In other words, it is important to the story that it is a *woman* caught in adultery. This is not merely a story of the *mercy* of Jesus toward a singular woman but also of the new *justice* he brings to the earth. His mercy overturns the stipulations of the law.

Moreover, if this passage originally belongs to the Gospel of John (some manuscripts place it in Luke's Gospel), then it is another example of the Johannine tendency to show Jesus in encounters with *individuals* (male or female) whose lives are forever changed by the encounter. Employing the plural for the sake of inclusivity contributes to deadening the true impact of the text.

The presider of the reconciliation service responded gratefully to the concerns I expressed after the service. But the incident reminded me again of the need for solid guidance in these questions. Proclaiming the Word of God is a serious pastoral responsibility. There are pastoral consequences for our understanding of the gospel message. Without proper guidance and without a solid effort from the Church's leaders to promote sensible guidelines on inclusive language, I fear we will promote a situation of liturgical anarchy. On the one side, those who despise any attempt to be inclusive will become more blatantly vigilante, trying to curb on their own authority any perceived change. On the other side, those who see inclusive language as a matter of justice will continue to make their own changes of texts in a haphazard and uninformed way that risks serious miscommunication of the gospel message. Neither approach does a service to the Church. Withdrawing the moderate and sensible approach to inclusive language from the public forum such as liturgy, where most Catholics experience their day-to-day faith, would only cause greater pastoral harm.

D. REMAINING QUESTIONS

By the time this book appears in print some of the issues raised in late 1994 may be resolved. Others may be relegated to ongoing discussion. Whatever the outcome, the following questions are some of the ones this latest controversy over inclusive language raises.

Are the concerns of the Roman congregations limited to the *NRSV* or is it really a matter of opposing all attempts at inclusive language in any translation?

If the concerns over inclusive language in the *NRSV* were truly *doctrinal*, how could Catholics logically still be encouraged to use it for private study and prayer but not for public worship or catechetics? If they are found to be stylistic, is there not a medium ground that can be agreed upon?

What does this controversy mean for the recently published (1993) Catholic edition of the *NRSV* that was published with an imprimatur?

What will happen to the American bishops' own guidelines on inclusive language? Will a new set of guidelines be forthcoming that will continue to promote a moderate approach to inclusive language?

What will happen to the revised translations of the *New American Bible,* commissioned by the American bishops precisely for a new lectionary? Will problems be raised about it because it employs inclusive language? Will this controversy lead to only one approved lectionary for English speaking countries, despite serious differences of linguistic usage in different English-speaking countries?

It is impossible to know where these and other questions may lead. There are those in the Church who will always resist any attempts to adapt the proclamation of the gospel to our own day. Adaptation properly done is not accommodation or dilution of the faith. It is a response to the signs of the times so that the faith may be communicated more understandably in our day. Despite the uncertainty that this recent controversy creates, I propose in the last chapter to summarize the essentials of inclusive language and to seek the challenge of the future.

Chapter V.

The Challenge of the Future

The guidelines given in this book are intended for use in local situations where other resources may be lacking. I emphasize again their interim nature and the desire that they help people in parishes understand the complexity of some of the issues. The guidelines will obviously not satisfy every instance in which exclusive/inclusive language is at issue, though they are applicable to various liturgical celebrations in addition to the Eucharist. Further research is continually being done and needs to be done by biblical, liturgical, and theological experts. As the previous chapter indicated, the hierarchy of the Church continues to explore this question and may make changes in the years ahead. These guidelines serve as interim "rules of thumb" to facilitate an effective and sensitive celebration of the liturgical life of the community under the current situation in which awareness of the issues is expanding but acceptable definitive alternatives are lacking.

I want to conclude this survey of the use of inclusive language in liturgy by means of a series of ten summary statements and a brief exposition of how our current situation leads to a renewed call to conversion.

A. Summary Statements

(1) *Language is vitally important.* The words we use not only mirror the attitudes we hold and the actions we perform, but they

also help create the reality around us. When I was a child I remember the saying, "Sticks and stones may break my bones, but words will never hurt me." But it wasn't true. Words can create a powerful hurt. Many people, women and men alike, know the destructive power of words as well as their constructive power. If virtually half of society experiences this kind of destructive power because of exclusive language, then something must be done so that our words reflect more appropriately the inclusive and healing nature of God's love for all humanity.

(2) *The issue of inclusive language is much more complicated than many people might realize.* Respecting inclusive language is not merely a matter of paging through the Lectionary or Sacramentary and excising perceived offensive language. Such a procedure is in serious danger historically, and theologically, of throwing the proverbial baby out with the bath water! For this reason, parish liturgists should be cautious. We must carefully weigh the implications of our decisions about language so that we do not squander our biblical and theological heritage.

(3) *Inclusive language is not a passing fancy of some unreasonable radicals out to destroy the Church.* Inclusive language is and will be for the future a necessity in society and the Church. As we have seen in many instances of proper biblical translation, the sense of the biblical and liturgical texts virtually requires attention to inclusive language in instances where the entire people of God, regardless of sex, are addressed. We can no longer allow our longstanding cultural prejudices to predetermine the way we wrestle with our patriarchal past.

(4) *Issues about inclusive language affect the lives of men and women alike.* Inclusivity is not restricted to women alone, nor are attempts to wrestle with exclusive language and history limited only to women. Inclusivity is an exercise in *human* liberation. It works for the dignity of all people regardless of sex, physical characteristics, racial or ethnic background, cultural history, language, and so on. The "liberation" of women consequently concerns the liberation of men as much as it concerns equality for women.

(5) *The biblical tradition witnesses to a history dominated by androcentrism.* The force and scope of androcentrism undervalued and overlooked what remained in the tradition of a feminine perspective. This imbalance can be and must be corrected by ap-

propriate attention to alternative biblical images that bring out of the shadows the inherent feminine dimensions of Scripture. The solution is not to rewrite history nor to deny its existence. The canonical status given the Scriptures requires that we wrestle with this patriarchal history and its impact on our own contemporary identity.

(6) *The communal nature of liturgy demands that all participants be included in the experience of worship.* This fundamental principle of liturgical celebration is a two-edged sword. On the one hand, it challenges parishes to be attentive to the need for inclusivity and for identifying and correcting elements that continue to promote exclusivity. On the other hand, the communal nature of liturgy also requires adherence to the Church's liturgical norms in order to prevent the use of liturgy as a platform for one's favorite pet peeves. The Church's liturgy is never *my* liturgy (this goes for the priests who preside at Eucharist as well), it is *ours* as a faith community. This means, of course, that the rights and responsibilities of the entire believing community take precedence over those of individuals.

(7) *Parish liturgists must inform themselves about the issues of inclusive language.* This applies equally to presiders and homilists, readers, musicians, liturgical planning committees, and any other personnel who have direct input into worship. Implied in this responsibility, and one of the basic purposes for this book, is the challenge of educating oneself in this area. Education and preparation go hand in hand and pave the way for more fruitful means of addressing inclusivity in the future.

(8) *An order of priorities exists with regard to what language can and should be changed in the liturgy.* There are certain limitations that I think we simply have to live with for the time being. While there is no excuse for allowing exclusive language to persist in areas of liturgy that refer to the assembly, I have indicated that some difficulties remain with attempts to make language about God or the Trinity be totally inclusive. Fortunately, as regards biblical readings, approved alternatives now exist for the current Lectionary and will be incorporated into the revised Lectionary whenever it is published.

(9) *Be patient with the slow pace of official change in the Church.* Keeping a historical perspective may help. The Church required several hundred years to recoup enough from the Reformation

to undergo the self-examination of conscience required of it in Vatican II. We are only some thirty years removed from that auspicious event that renewed the life of the Church in so many ways. Those who want their inclusive language *now* in every aspect of societal or ecclesial life are being unrealistic. I am convinced that the issue is so widely recognized now, albeit in a grudging fashion at times, that the road has been firmly set for the future. Change will happen, and I believe it will happen under the guidance of the Holy Spirit, much as the Spirit has always guided the Church (illustrated so well in the Acts of the Apostles). As handmaids of patience, faith, hope, and love are also necessary in this endeavor to work toward greater inclusivity.

(10) *Language alone will not be the solution to inclusivity.* As important and symbolic as language is, it reflects deeper realities in which the liberation of both women and men is at stake. Structural changes in society and in the Church are without doubt necessary to address the exclusivity that so many women experience in their lives. But I suggest that no one has *the* solution readily at hand that can help us remain faithful to our biblical and historical traditions while working toward a truly just and equal society. The attempts to move beyond stereotypes in our language will have to be accompanied by struggles over the very shape of our daily lives.

B. CALL TO CONVERSION

Taking seriously the interim nature of the proposals in this book can serve as a reminder that the controversies and tensions surrounding inclusive language are symbolic of the need for ongoing conversion in the life of the Church. Exclusivity in word or in deed is a sign that God's reign has not *fully* come upon us and that we do not incarnate God's values totally in our lives. At the center of the New Testament notion of conversion is the necessity of changing one's mind (from the Greek, *metanoia*).[75] Re-

---

75. For a more complete exposition of the New Testament notion of conversion, see Ronald D. Witherup, *Conversion in the New Testament*, Zacchaeus Studies New Testament (Collegeville, Minn.: The Liturgical Press, 1994).

sistance to conversion is often that: refusal to change one's mind. Even disciples of Jesus must continue to be changed over and over again by God's grace. John Henry Newman, one of the Church's great models of ongoing conversion, wrote in his book, *An Essay on the Development of Christian Doctrine,* an often quoted line: "In a higher world it is otherwise, but here below to live is to change, and to be perfect is to have changed often." Elsewhere in one of his sermons he indicates just how difficult the change necessary for conversion is:

> We do not like to be new-made; we are afraid of it; it is throwing us out of all our natural ways, of all that is familiar to us. We feel as if we should not *be* ourselves any longer, if we do not keep some portion of what we have been hitherto; and much as we prefer in general terms to wish to be changed, when it comes to the point, when particular instances of change are presented to us, we shrink from them, and are content to remain unchanged.[76]

We may resist the change, and when it comes to inclusive language we must make changes carefully, but at the heart of this endeavor is nothing less than a call to Christian conversion in order to create a world that embraces all humanity.

Many will not be satisfied because these guidelines do not go far enough or are too timid to make a difference. The pace of change in the Church is often painfully slow. Still others may reject outright any suggestion that the guidelines be used because they do not want to concede at all the need for inclusive language. The purpose of this book has been to acknowledge that this issue is one of such vital importance that it must be addressed, even while we await more definitive solutions to these complex problems.[77] The interim nature of the guidelines does not mean paralysis. I urge those working with liturgy on the parochial level to get involved in this issue, to study it and learn more about it, and to act on it *responsibly* within the constraints of the current situation.

76. Quoted in Ian Ker, *Newman on Being a Christian* (Notre Dame, Ind.: University of Notre Dame, 1990) 132.

77. One notes the cautious but insistent tone expressed by the Roman Catholic bishops of Canada in their pastoral message, "To Speak as a Christian Community," *Origins* 19 (September 21, 1989) 258–260.

I have argued throughout this book the necessity of great caution in this area, especially with regard to the Bible, because of the serious risks involved in naive or uninformed linguistic changes. The Church itself has taken the cautious approach, as is seen in the Pontifical Biblical Commission's recent document on biblical interpretation.[78] The Commission both commends and cautions trends in feminist biblical interpretation. From a positive perspective, the document notes:

> Feminist exegesis has brought many benefits. Women have played a more active part in exegetical research. They have succeeded, often better than men, in detecting the presence, the significance and the role of women in the Bible, in Christian origins and in the church. . . . Feminine sensitivity helps to unmask and correct certain commonly accepted interpretations which were tendentious and sought to justify the male domination of women.[79]

On the other hand, the document warns against excesses in biblical interpretation that are based on hypothetical reconstructions or exaggerated interpretations, or that fall into the trap of using interpretation merely as an exercise in power. "Feminist exegesis . . . can be useful to the church only to the degree that it does not fall into the very traps it denounces and that it does not lose sight of the evangelical teaching concerning power as service, a teaching addressed by Jesus to all disciples, men and women" (p. 509).

One liturgical theologian has summarized this need for caution well especially as it pertains to public worship. In the context of the rapid changes experienced in culture in the late twentieth century, Geoffrey Wainwright points out a rationale for

---

78. "The Interpretation of the Bible in the Church," *Origins* 23:29 (January 6, 1994) 497–524. This document was approved and highly commended by Pope John Paul II in April 1993 on the occasion of the anniversaries of two major encyclicals on biblical interpretation, Leo XIII's "Providentissimus Deus" (1893) and Pius XII's "Divino afflante Spiritu" (1943). For a summary, see Ronald D. Witherup, "A New *Magna Carta* for Catholic Biblical Studies?" *BToday* 32 (1994) 336–341, and "Is There a Catholic Approach to the Bible?" *The Priest* 51:2 (1995) 29–35.

79. *Origins* 23:29 (1994) 509.

a cautious approach. Although these words were formulated more than a decade ago when inclusive language issues were just emerging, I think they also apply to the situation today regarding such language.

> At this time, therefore, it is important that official liturgical revision should err on the conservative side, if the faith is to be transmitted through a period of reductionism into a time when an adequate reformulation of its substance may take place. It is never a function of *avant-garde* theologians to control the public worship of the Church. The "theology" expressed in official worship must be acceptable to the broadest possible range in the present Christian community and must be as faithful as possible to what is sensed to be authentic in the past. That is because the liturgy is a public act by which the worshipers identify themselves with a continuing community and enter into the "story" of that community.[80]

In many ways what inclusive language is all about is unity and equality. Previously I invoked St. Paul and his call to the Corinthian community to resist their urge to be divisive and to reestablish their unity in Christ, because of their equality in baptism. I visit that image again in closing. St. Paul has often been castigated (wrongly and anachronistically in my opinion) as a misogynist. As we noted above, there are some troubling texts in the Pauline literature. But in concluding this foray into the theological world of biblical and liturgical language, I can think of no person in the New Testament who more eloquently speaks numerous times about the need for unity in the Church (see 1 Corinthians especially). In fact, this sentiment about the need for unity is a driving force behind calling for a cautious approach to inclusive language. Although some have already opted to leave the Church because they see it as a hopelessly patriarchal system beyond repair, I am fearful of even greater needless disunity over issues that are poorly understood and inefficiently communicated. Language can become an even greater tool for division in the Church than

---

80. *Doxology: The Praise of God in Worship, Doctrine, and Life* (New York: Oxford University, 1980) 344. Another voice that echoes this sentiment more recently with regard to language is George T. Montague, "Freezing the Fire: The Death of Relational Language," *America* 168:9 (March 13, 1993) 5–7.

it has already been.[81] We do not need more avenues to drive the wedge of division further into the Body of Christ. We need new ways to foster a true unity that respects the dignity of each daughter or son of God equally. A primary purpose of liturgy is to celebrate the deeper unity (not always apparent) we have in Christ Jesus and to foster a greater incarnation of that unity in our daily lives. Liturgy itself, then, must struggle to create as much unity as possible rather than disunity. These interim guidelines are only a tiny step toward a greater inclusivity that will one day come. In the meantime, perhaps all can pray that some day the words of St. Paul may have their full effect in each of our lives:

> For in Christ Jesus you are all children of God through faith. As many of you as were baptized into Christ have clothed yourselves with Christ. There is no longer Jew or Greek, there is no longer slave or free, there is no longer male and female; for all of you are one in Christ Jesus (Gal 3:26-28; cf. 1 Cor 12:13; Col 3:11).

81. See Pope John Paul II's comments, *Origins* 23:8 (July 15, 1993) 126.

Glossary

The following definitions apply to technical terms used in this book and do not represent universal meanings of these terms.

analogical language: the use of analogies to describe God; this includes similes and metaphors, and all language that represents or describes God in ways beyond literal meaning.

androcentrism: making characteristics of men (as compared to women) the central, normative system of society

anthropomorphism: the use of human behavior, motivations, and emotions to characterize God

exclusive language: language that distinguishes one group or type of people and excludes others; most restrictively this expression refers to "sexist" language that exalts men and excludes or puts down women

gender: refers to the different ways in which people experience their sexual identity as male or female, that is, the notions of "masculine" and "feminine" as determined by culture.

horizontal inclusive language: language descriptive of human beings that embraces both female and male perspectives

inclusive language: language that attempts in a neutral way to include all people, regardless of race, ethnicity, sex, creed, age, or physical characteristics; most restrictively this expression refers to gender-neutral language that views women and men equally.

misogyny: literally, the hatred of women; this term applies to discrimination against women throughout history solely on the basis of their sex

patriarchy: the system of tracing ancestry through male lineage; this term represents the cultural and biblical bias of favoring the male perspective over that of females

sex: the biological reality of being male or female

sexism: the use of biological sex, consciously or unconsciously, to exalt one sex over the other; this word is usually understood as implying male domination over women

vertical inclusive language: language descriptive of God that embraces both female and male perspectives

Appendix:
The American Bishops' Guidelines

This appendix reprints with permission the guidelines on inclusive language developed and approved by the American bishops in 1990. Although they were intended for use by official bible translators and bishops, I have used them throughout this book to illustrate both the need for caution *and* the need for proper use of inclusive language with regard to biblical translations and liturgical texts. The guidelines are published here for the convenient reference of the reader. The original edition is available from USCC Publishing Services ([800]-235-8722).

CRITERIA FOR THE EVALUATION OF INCLUSIVE LANGUAGE TRANSLATIONS OF SCRIPTURAL TEXTS PROPOSED FOR LITURGICAL USE

© 1990 United States Catholic Conference, Washington, D.C.)

Introduction: Origins and Nature of the Problem

1. Five historical developments have converged to present the church in the United States today with an important and challenging pastoral concern. First, the introduction of the vernacular into the church's worship has necessitated English translations of the

liturgical books and of sacred Scripture for use in the liturgy. Second, some segments of American culture have become increasingly sensitive to "exclusive language," i.e., language which seems to exclude the equality and dignity of each person regardless of race, gender, creed, age or ability.[1] Third, there has been a noticeable loss of the sense of grammatical gender in American usage of the English language. Fourth, English vocabulary itself has changed so that words which once referred to all human beings are increasingly taken as gender specific and, consequently, exclusive. Fifth, impromptu efforts at inclusive language, while pleasing to some, have often offended others who expect a degree of theological precision and linguistic or aesthetic refinement in the public discourse of the liturgy. Some impromptu efforts may also have unwittingly undermined essentials of Catholic doctrine.

These current issues confront a fundamental conviction of the church, namely, that the word of God stands at the core of our faith as a basic theological reality to which all human efforts respond and by which they are judged.

2. The bishops of the United States wish to respond to this complex and sensitive issue of language in the English translation of the liturgical books of the church in general and of sacred Scripture in particular. New translations of scriptural passages used in the liturgy are being proposed periodically for their approval. Since the promulgation of the 1983 Code of Canon Law, these translations must be approved by a conference of bishops or by the Apostolic See.[2] The question confronts the bishops: With regard to a concern for inclusive language, how do we distinguish a legitimate translation from one that is imprecise?

3. The recognition of this problem prompted the submission of a varium to the National Conference of Catholic Bishops requesting that the bishops' Committee on the Liturgy and the Committee on Doctrine be directed jointly to formulate guidelines which would assist the bishops in making appropriate judgments on the inclusive-language translations of biblical texts for liturgical use. These two committees established a joint committee on inclusive language, which prepared this text.

---

[1] Cf. Bishop Members of the Pastoral Team, Canadian Conference of Catholic Bishops, *To Speak as a Christian Community* (Aug. 16, 1989), p. 2.

[2] Code of Canon Law, Canon 825.1.

4. This document, while providing an answer to the question concerning translations of biblical texts for liturgical use, does not attempt to elaborate a complete set of criteria for inclusive language in the liturgy in general, that is, for prayers, hymns and preaching. These cognate areas will be treated only insofar as they overlap the particular issues being addressed here.

5. This document presents practical principles for the members of the National Conference of Catholic Bishops to exercise their canonical responsibility for approving translations of Scripture proposed for liturgical use. However, just as this document does not deal with all cases of inclusive language in the liturgy, neither is it intended as a theology of translation. The teaching of *Dei Verbum* and the instructions of the Pontifical Biblical Commission prevail in matters of inspiration, inerrancy and hermeneutics and their relationship with meaning, language and the mind of the author. While there would be a value in producing a study summarizing these issues, it would distract from the immediate purpose of this document.

6. This document treats the problem indicated above in four parts: general principles; principles for inclusive-language lectionary translations; preparation of texts for use in the lectionary; special questions, viz., naming God, the Trinity, Christ and the church.

Part I
General Principles

7. There are two general principles for judging translations for liturgical use: the principle of fidelity to the word of God and the principle of respect for the nature of the liturgical assembly. Individual questions, then, must be judged in light of the textual, grammatical, literary, artistic and dogmatic requirements of the particular scriptural passage and in light of the needs of the liturgical assembly. In cases of conflict or ambiguity, the principle of fidelity to the word of God retains its primacy.

I. FIDELITY TO THE WORD OF GOD

The following considerations derive from the principle of fidelity to the word of God.

8. The people of God have the right to hear the word of God integrally proclaimed[3] in fidelity to the meaning of the inspired authors of the sacred text.

9. Biblical translations must always be faithful to the original language and internal truth of the inspired text. It is expected, therefore, that every concept in the original text will be translated within its context.

10. All biblical translations must respect doctrinal principles of revelation, inspiration and biblical interpretation (hermeneutics) as well as the formal rhetoric intended by the author (e.g., Heb. 2:5-18). They must be faithful to Catholic teaching regarding God and divine activity in the world and in human history as it unfolds. "Due attention must be paid both to the customary and characteristic patterns of perception, speech and narrative which prevailed at the age of the sacred writer and to the conventions which the people of his time followed."[4]

II. The Nature of the Liturgical Assembly

The following considerations derive from the nature of the liturgical assembly.

11. Each and every Christian is called to and indeed has a right to full and active participation in worship. This was stated succinctly by the Second Vatican Council: "The church earnestly desires that all the faithful be led to that full, conscious and active participation in liturgical celebrations called for by the very nature of the liturgy. Such participation by the Christian people as 'a chosen race, a royal priesthood, a holy nation, God's own people' (I Pt. 2:9, see 2:4-5) is their right and duty by reason of their baptism."[5] An integral part of liturgical participation is hearing the word of Christ, "who speaks when the Scriptures are proclaimed in the church."[6] Full and active participation in the liturgy demands that the liturgical assembly recognize and accept the transcendent power of God's word.

[3] Canon 213.

[4] Vatican Council II, Dogmatic Constitution on Divine Revelation, 12.

[5] Ibid., Constitution on the Sacred Liturgy, 14. English translation is from *Documents on the Liturgy 1963–1979: Conciliar, Papal and Curial Texts* (hereafter DOL) (Collegeville, Minn: The Liturgical Press, 1982), 1, 14.

[6] Ibid., 7.

12. According to the church's tradition, biblical texts have many liturgical uses. Because their immediate purposes are somewhat different, texts translated for public proclamation in the liturgy may differ in some respects (cf. Part 2) from those translations which are meant solely for academic study, private reading or *lectio divina*.

13. The language of biblical texts for liturgical use should be suitable and faithfully adapted for proclamation and should facilitate the full, conscious and active participation of all members of the church, women and men, in worship.

Part 2
Principles for Inclusive-Language Lectionary Translation

14. The word of God proclaimed to all nations is by nature inclusive that is, addressed to all peoples, men and women. Consequently, every effort should be made to render the language of biblical translations as inclusively as a faithful translation of the text permits, especially when this concerns the people of God, Israel and the Christian community.

15. When a biblical translation is meant for liturgical proclamation, it must also take into account those principles which apply to the public communication of the biblical meaning. Inclusive language is one of those principles, since the text is proclaimed in the Christian assembly to women and men who possess equal baptismal dignity and reflects the universal scope of the church's call to evangelize.

16. The books of the Bible are the product of particular cultures, with their limitations as well as their strengths. Consequently not everything in Scripture will be in harmony with contemporary cultural concerns. The fundamental mystery of incarnational revelation requires the retention of those characteristics which reflect the cultural context within which the word was first received.

17. Language which addresses and refers to the worshiping community ought not use words or phrases which deny the common dignity of all the baptized.

18. Words such as *men, sons, brothers, brethren, forefathers, fraternity* and *brotherhood,* which were once understood as inclusive generic terms, today are often understood as referring only to males. In addition, although certain uses of *he, his* and *him* once were generic and included both men and women, in contemporary American usage these terms are often perceived to refer only to males. Their use has become ambiguous and is increasingly seen to exclude women. Therefore, these terms should not be used when the reference is meant to be generic, observing the requirements of No. 7 and No. 10.

19. Words such as *'adam, anthropos* and *homo* have often been translated in many English biblical and liturgical texts by the collective terms *man* and *family of man.* Since in the original languages these words actually denote human beings rather than only males, English terms which are not gender specific, such as *person, people, human family* and *humans,* should be used in translating these words.

20. In narratives and parables the sex of individual persons should be retained. Sometimes, in the synoptic tradition, the Gospel writers select examples or metaphors from a specific gender. Persons of the other sex should not be added merely in a desire for balance. The original references of the narrative or images of the parable should be retained.

Part 3
Preparation of Texts for Use in the Lectionary

21. The liturgical adaptation of readings for use in the lectionary should be made in light of the norms of the introduction to the *Ordo Lectionum Missae* (1981). Incipits should present the context of the various pericopes. At times, transitions may need to be added when verses have been omitted from pericopes. Nouns may replace pronouns or be added to participial constructions for clarity in proclamation and aural comprehension. Translation should not expand upon the text, but the church recognizes that in certain circumstances a particular text may be expanded to reflect adequately the intended meaning of the pericope.[7] In all

[7] Secretariat for Christian Unity (Commission for Religious Relations With Judaism), "Guidelines and Suggestions for the Application of No. 14 of the

cases, these adaptations must remain faithful to the intent of the original text.[8]

22. Inclusive-language adaptations of lectionary texts must be made in light of exegetical and linguistic attention to the individual text within its proper context. Blanket substitutions are inappropriate.

23. Many biblical passages are inconsistent in grammatical person, that is, alternating between second person singular or plural *(you)* and third person singular *(he)*. In order to give such passages a more intelligible consistency, some biblical readings may be translated so as to use either the second person plural *(you)* throughout or the third person plural *(they)* throughout. Changes from the third person singular to the third person plural are allowed in individual cases where the sense of the original text is universal. It should be noted that, at times, either the sense or the poetic structure of a passage may require that the alternation be preserved in the translation.

24. Psalms and canticles have habitually been appropriated by the church for use in the liturgy, not as readings for proclamation, but as the responsive prayer of the liturgical assembly. Accordingly, adaptations have justifiably been made, principally by the omission of verses which were judged to be inappropriate in a given culture or liturgical context. Thus, the liturgical books allow the adaptation of psalm texts to encourage the full participation of the liturgical assembly.

Part 4
Special Questions

25. Several specific issues must be addressed in regard to the naming of God, the persons of the Trinity and the church, since changes in language can have important doctrinal and theological implications.

Conciliar Declaration *Nostra Aetate,*" Oct. 28, 1975 (AAS 67 [1975] 73–79).

[8] Sacred Congregation of Rites (Consilium), instruction *Comme le Prevoit* on the translation of liturgical texts for celebrations with a congregation (Jan. 25, 1969) (DOL 123), 30–32.

I. NAMING GOD IN BIBLICAL TRANSLATIONS

26. Great care should be taken in translations of the names of God and in the use of pronouns referring to God. While it would be inappropriate to attribute gender to God as such, the revealed word of God consistently uses a masculine reference for God. It may sometimes be useful, however, to repeat the name of God as used earlier in the text rather than to use the masculine pronoun in every case. But care must be taken that the repetition not become tiresome.

27. The classic translation of the Tetragrammaton (YHWH) as *LORD* and the translation of *Kyrios* as *Lord* should be used in lectionaries.

28. Feminine imagery in the original language of the biblical texts should not be obscured or replaced by the use of masculine imagery in English translations, e.g., Wisdom literature.

II. NAMING CHRIST IN BIBLICAL TRANSLATIONS

29. Christ is the center and focus of all Scripture.[9] The New Testament has interpreted certain texts of the Old Testament in an explicitly Christological fashion. Special care should be observed in the translation of these texts so that the Christological meaning is not lost. Some examples include the Servant Songs of Isaiah 42 and 53, Psalms 2 and 110, and the Son of Man passage in Daniel 7.

III. NAMING THE TRINITY IN BIBLICAL TRANSLATIONS

30. In fidelity to the inspired word of God, the traditional biblical usage for naming the Persons of the Trinity as *Father, Son* and *Holy Spirit* is to be retained. Similarly, in keeping with New Testament usage and the church's tradition, the feminine pronoun is not to be used to refer to the Person of the Holy Spirit.

IV. NAMING THE CHURCH IN BIBLICAL TRANSLATIONS

31. Normally the neuter third person singular or the third person plural pronoun is used when referring to the people of God, Israel, the church, the body of Christ, etc., unless their antecedents

[9] Cf. Dogmatic Constitution on Divine Revelation, 16.

clearly are a masculine or feminine metaphor, for instance, the reference to the church as the bride of Christ or mother (cf. Rv. 12).

Conclusion

32. These criteria for judging the appropriateness of inclusive-language translations of sacred Scripture are presented while acknowledging that the English language is continually changing. Contemporary translations must reflect developments in American English grammar, syntax, usage, vocabulary and style. The perceived need for a more inclusive language is part of this development. Such language must not distract hearers from prayer and God's revelation. It must manifest a sense of linguistic refinement. It should not draw attention to itself.

33. While English translations of the Bible have influenced the liturgical and devotional language of Christians such translations have also shaped and formed the English language itself. This should be true today as it was in the age of the King James and Douay-Rheims translations. Thus, the church expects for its translations not only accuracy but facility and beauty of expression.

34. Principles of translation when applied to lectionary readings and psalm texts differ in certain respects from those applied to translations of the Bible destined for study or reading (see Nos. 22–25 above). Thus when submitting a new or revised translation of the Bible, an edition of the lectionary or a liturgical psalter for approval by the National Conference of Catholic Bishops, editors must supply a complete statement of the principles used in the preparation of the submitted text.

35. The authority to adapt the biblical text for use in the lectionary remains with the conference of bishops. These criteria for the evaluation of Scripture translations proposed for use in the liturgy have been developed to assist the members of the National Conference of Catholic Bishops to exercise their responsibility so that all the people of God may be assisted in hearing God's word and keeping it.

Selected Annotated Bibliography
for Further Reading

Publications in this area are burgeoning at such a rapid pace that it is nearly impossible to keep current. The following publications have been chosen (in addition to those listed in the footnotes) for their usefulness to liturgists in a parochial situation who wish to study the issue of inclusive language in greater depth. To that end materials are organized according to two categories, feminist theological and biblical issues in general and inclusive language issues in particular, although there is inevitably some overlap. Entries marked with an asterisk (*) indicate resources I recommend as good introductory materials for those who have little background in this topic.

RESOURCES FOR FEMINIST THEOLOGY AND BIBLICAL INTERPRETATION IN GENERAL

Aldredge-Clanton, Jann. *In Search of the Christ-Sophia: An Inclusive Christology for Liberating Christians.* Mystic, Conn.: Twenty-Third Publications, 1995. A serious attempt by a Baptist minister to explore the biblical and theological foundations of the wisdom tradition to develop a more liberating and inclusive Christology.

Anderson, Janice Capel. "Mapping Feminist Biblical Criticism: The American Scene, 1983–1990." *Critical Review of Books in Religion, 1991 Annual.* (AAR/SBL). A scholarly review of recent feminist biblical studies, where it has come from and where it is going.

Benjamin, Don C. "Israel's God: Mother and Midwife." *BTB* 19 (1989) 115–120. An exploration of the feminine dimensions of God in the Old Testament from the sociological perspective of the history and role of the midwife.

Demers, Patricia. *Women as Interpreters of the Bible.* New York: Paulist, 1992. A historical overview of how women have interpreted the Scriptures from medieval times to the present.

Dewey, Joanna. "Feminist Readings, Gospel Narrative and Critical Theory." *BTB* 22 (1992) 167–173. An article in dialogue with other scholars about the nature of contemporary biblical interpretation, especially from a feminist perspective; includes further bibliography on interpretation.

*Hamerton-Kelly, Robert. *God the Father: Theology and Patriarchy in the Teaching of Jesus.* Philadelphia: Fortress, 1979. A very readable scholarly examination of the New Testament's use of "father language."

Interpretation 42:1 (1988). The entire issue is devoted to concerns in feminist theology, with articles by K. D. Sakenfeld, E. A. Achtemeier, G. Stroup, and P. Perkins.

Johnson, Elizabeth A. "Feminist Hermeneutics." *Chicago Studies* 27 (1988) 123–135. A good overview of the rationale and issues involved in feminist biblical interpretation; outlines presuppositions and strategies for liberationist methods of interpretation.

_____. *She Who Is: The Mystery of God in Feminist Theological Discourse.* New York: Crossroad, 1992. This award-winning book offers one of the most sophisticated analyses of Trinitarian issues from a feminist perspective currently available.

Kay, James F. "In Whose Name? Feminism and the Trinitarian Baptismal Formula." *TToday* 49 (1993) 524–533. A critique of one feminist's call to abandon Trinitarian language (Ruth C. Duck. *Gender and the Name of God: The Trinitarian Baptismal Formula.* New York: Pilgrim, 1991). Kay feels such language has important ecumenical implications and should not be lightly cast off.

Lardner Carmody, Denise. *Biblical Woman: Contemporary Reflections on Scriptural Texts.* New York: Crossroad, 1988. An interesting exploration of various Old and New Testament texts on women, including many texts that women find problematic. This book is intended for college students and those in adult education classes, and each chapter is accompanied by a few pertinent discussion questions.

Miller, John W. "Depatriarchalizing God in Biblical Interpretation: A Critique." *CBQ* 48 (1986) 609–616. A brief and careful scholarly critique of feminist overinterpretation of some biblical passages.

Martin, Francis. "Feminist Hermeneutics: An Overview, Part I." *Communio* 18 (1991) 144–163.

_____. "Feminist Hermeneutics: An Overview, Part II." *Communio* 18 (1991) 398–424. Both of these articles contain an extensive analysis and critique of contemporary feminist biblical interpretation. Provides good summary material and extensive bibliography. These articles are expanded in the author's book, *The Feminist Question: Feminist Theology in Light of Christian Tradition.* Grand Rapids: Eerdmans, 1994.

*Milne, Pamela J. "Feminist Interpretations of the Bible: Then and Now." *BR* 8:5 (1992) 38–43, 52–55. A good succinct historical treatment of feminist biblical interpretation.

*Moloney, Francis J. *Woman First Among the Faithful: A New Testament Study.* Notre Dame, Ind.: Ave Maria, 1986. A good discussion of the New Testament portrayal of women, especially in Paul, the Gospels of Matthew, Luke and John, and the Book of Revelation; shows the significant roles women played in the New Testament period despite tendencies to downplay them.

Murphy, Cullen. "Women and the Bible." *Atlantic Monthly* 272:2 (August 1993) 39–64. An overview of current biblical research on the role of women in the Bible based upon the work of several women scholars and written for a general popular audience.

*Osiek, Carolyn. *Beyond Anger: On Being a Feminist in the Church.* New York: Paulist, 1986. A broad treatment for general audiences of feminist issues in Roman Catholicism; tries to respond to the often hurtful experiences of women in the Church.

Podles, Mary and Leon J. Podles. "The Emasculation of God." *America* 161 (November 25, 1989) 372–374. A provocative article on the maleness of Christ seen throughout history (especially in art) and our discomfort with that image.

Procter-Smith, Marjorie. *In Her Own Rite: Constructing Feminist Liturgical Tradition.* Nashville: Abingdon, 1990. A passionately argued approach to feminist perspectives in Christian liturgical life, with two chapters specifically devoted to language.

*Ramey Mollenkott, Virginia. *The Divine Feminine: The Biblical Imagery of God as Female.* New York: Crossroad, 1989. A good, balanced book-length treatment of the feminine imagery for God in the Bible.

*_____. *Women, Men, and the Bible.* Rev. ed. New York: Crossroad, 1988. A broad introductory survey of issues in Christian feminism and biblical interpretation intended for general audiences and accompanied by a study guide for discussions.

*Rosenblatt, Marie-Eloise, ed. *Where Can We Find Her? Searching for Women's Identity in the New Church.* New York/Mahwah: Paulist, 1991. A collection of essays from Roman Catholic women theologians from various theological disciplines. The final chapter includes a discussion guide for group leaders that can be used in adult enrichment settings.

Routley, Erik. "The Gender of God: A Contribution to the Conversation." *Worship* 56 (1982) 231–239. An application of the issues of inclusive language to Christian hymns.

Ruether, Rosemary Radford, ed. *Religion and Sexism: Images of Woman in the Jewish and Christian Traditions.* New York: Simon & Schuster, 1974. A collection of scholarly essays on the images of woman in Jewish and Christian traditions. This book goes beyond analysis of the biblical data but includes discussion of Old Testament and New Testament texts.

_____. *Sexism and God-Talk: Toward a Feminist Theology.* Boston: Beacon, 1983. A bold, creative, and influential exploration of many aspects of theology from a feminist perspective, reissued in 1993 (with a new preface) on the tenth anniversary of its publication.

Russell, Letty M., ed. *Feminist Interpretation of the Bible.* Philadelphia: Westminster, 1985. A broad collection of essays by prominent feminist scholars from the AAR/SBL, covering historical, biblical, and theological issues.

*Schneiders, Sandra M. *Beyond Patching: Faith and Feminism in the Catholic Church.* New York: Paulist, 1991. A very good introduction for lay people to the practice of feminist hermeneutics.

*_____. "Feminist Ideology Criticism and Biblical Hermeneutics." *BTB* 19 (1989) 3–10. A brief but sophisticated overview of the feminist approach to the Bible, especially regarding texts that seem intrinsically oppressive.

*_____. *Women and the Word.* New York: Paulist, 1986. Originally a Madeleva Lecture delivered at St. Mary's College (Notre Dame, Ind.), this is an excellent essay about the gender of God and how it relates to women.

Schüssler Fiorenza, Elisabeth. *Bread Not Stone: The Challenge of Feminist Biblical Interpretation.* Boston: Beacon, 1985. A scholarly book of essays, most of them previously published in journals, collected for further illustration of feminist biblical interpretation.

_____. *But She Said: Feminist Practices of Biblical Interpretation.* Boston: Beacon, 1992. Another application of the author's method of interpreting biblical texts from her feminist perspective, focusing on specific women and texts in the Bible.

_____. *In Memory of Her: A Feminist Reconstruction of Christian Origins.* New York: Crossroad, 1983. An important scholarly and groundbreaking book in the area of feminist hermeneutics, unfortunately marred by what some scholars would consider overinterpretation of biblical texts. Her concept of a "hermeneutics of suspicion" calls for rereading the Bible to expose the ways in which the role of women was obscured by the patriarchal biblical tradition.

Swidler, Leonard. "God, Father and Mother." *BToday* 22 (1984) 300–305. A very brief look at the theme of the feminine and masculine dimension of God in the Bible.

Trible, Phyllis. *God and the Rhetoric of Sexuality.* Philadelphia: Fortress, 1978.

*————. "If the Bible's So Patriarchal, How Come I Love It?" *BR* 8:5 (1992) 44–47, 55. A balanced perspective of both the pain and the joy of reading the Bible as a woman biblical scholar.

————. *Texts of Terror: Literary-Feminist Readings of Biblical Narratives.* Philadelphia: Fortress, 1984. This book and *God and the Rhetoric of Sexuality* are well researched and thoughtful interpretations of Old Testament texts, especially those about women, based upon rhetorical features of the original language.

Yarbro Collins, Adela, ed. *Feminist Perspectives in Biblical Scholarship.* Chico, Calif.: Scholars, 1985. A collection of scholarly essays by contemporary feminist biblical interpreters.

RESOURCES FOR INCLUSIVE LANGUAGE

*Aldredge Clanton, Jann. *In Whose Image? God and Gender.* New York: Crossroad, 1992. An excellent introduction to inclusive language issues; written by a Southern Baptist minister but with ecumenical sensitivities. Each chapter includes a set of discussion questions, and the appendix contains a "Religious Opinion Survey" used to help surface attitudes toward issues of inclusivity.

Baron, Dennis. *Grammar and Gender.* New Haven and London: Yale University Press, 1986. A sophisticated historical study of the English language that demonstrates how grammar and culture are closely tied together. The author, a professor of English and Linguistics at the University of Illinois, also recounts the history of sexual bias in the English language and various attempts at reform. This work clearly debunks any notion that the search for inclusive language is merely a "modern" concern. The search for a more common pronoun for both males and females (the "epicene pronoun") has existed since the time of "Middle English."

Bird, Phyllis A. "Translating Sexist Language as a Theological and Cultural Problem." *USQR* 42 (1988) 89–95. A scholarly attempt to expose the androcentric and patriarchal nature of biblical texts and the necessity of understanding them in their original setting and purpose.

*Bloesch, Donald G. *Is the Bible Sexist?* Westchester, Ill.: Crossway, 1982. An attempt to combat more extreme forms of feminist biblical and theological interpretation while fostering inclusivity through the notion of God's covenant of grace with men and women.

Collins, Mary. "Glorious Praise: The ICEL Liturgical Psalter." *Worship* 66 (1992) 290–310. A report on the vision and process of translation of the ICEL liturgical psalter.

_____. "Naming God in Public Prayer." *Worship* 59 (1985) 291–304. A survey of options on ways to address God in settings of public worship and on the rediscovery of feminine metaphors for God.

Fogarty, Gerald P. " 'The English Used in Our Country.' Bible Translations for U.S. Catholics." *America* 172:7 (March 4, 1995) 10–16. Written by a prominent Church historian, this article demonstrates how controversies over Bible translations are paralleled in American Church history.

Frye, Roland Mushat. "Language for God and Feminist Language: A Literary and Rhetorical Analysis." *Interpretation* 43 (1989) 45–57. Argues that some attempts to employ alternative images for God can lead to linguistic, literary, theological, and historical distortions of the biblical tradition.

Gaffney, James. "She Who Laughs Last: The Gender-Inclusive Language Debate." *America* 173:5 (Aug. 26–Sept. 2, 1995) 8–12. This is a thoughtful account of how the author has gradually grown in awareness of the need for gender-inclusive language. Gaffney argues for a seldom appreciated moral dimension of the question.

Groome, Thomas H. *Language for a "Catholic" Church.* 2d ed. Kansas City: Sheed & Ward, 1995. A brief introduction to inclusive-language issues in the Roman Catholic context. Includes questions for further dialogue and discussion.

*Hardesty, Nancy A. *Inclusive Language in the Church.* Atlanta: John Knox, 1987. A judicious treatment of the subject that avoids strident positions while passionately calling for inclusive language. Lacks discussion of Roman Catholic liturgical settings.

Hook, Donald D., and Alvin F. Kimel, Jr. "Forum: Is God a 'He'?" *Worship* 68 (1994) 145–157. Using the basic arguments from the essay "The Pronouns of Diety: A Theolinguistic Critique of Feminist Proposals" in a more streamlined manner, the same two authors emphasize grammatical reasons for retaining masculine language for God.

_____. "The Pronouns of Deity: A Theolinguistic Critique of Feminist Proposals." *SJT* 46 (1993) 297–323. This essay argues that English grammar and syntax require retaining masculine language for describing God and that such language does not force a gender-specific identification of God as male. It also critiques specific alternative proposals of some feminist scholars.

Hurd, Robert L. "Complementarity: A Proposal for Liturgical Language." *Worship* 61 (1987) 386–405. Proposes the notion of complementarity in the sense of "co-equal," rather than inclusivity, as the basis for changes in liturgical language.

*Jensen, Joseph. "Inclusive Language and the Bible." *America* 171:14 (November 5, 1994) 14–18. An articulate defense of the need for inclusive language in contemporary American Bible translations. The backdrop for this article was the controversy that developed in October 1994 over the use of the *NRSV* in worship and catechesis.

Kimel, Alvin F. Jr., ed. *Speaking the Christian God: The Holy Trinity and the Challenge of Feminism.* Grand Rapids: Eerdmans, 1992. An extensive collection of essays from various Christian scholars proposing a strong critique of the attempts of feminist theologians to redefine the Trinity and to grapple with the Christian understanding of God.

*Montague, George T. "Freezing the Fire: The Death of Rational Language." *America* 168:9 (March 13, 1993) 5–7. A plea for caution and moderation in the desire to change father language for God.

*Oxford-Carpenter, R. "Gender and the Trinity." *TToday* 41 (1984) 7–25. A good overview of Trinitarian language in the Bible and the history of theology; argues for the use of multiple metaphors incorporating personal and nonpersonal, female and male imagery for the Trinity.

Payne Allen, Pamela. "Taking the Next Step in Inclusive Language." *Christian Century* 103 (April 23, 1986) 410–413. A practical article by a director of music arguing for the need to employ feminine imagery for God in liturgy and hymnody in order to redress the wrongs of patriarchy.

Ramshaw, Gail. *God beyond Gender: Feminist Christian God-Language.* Minneapolis: Fortress Press, 1995. A well reasoned attempt within the Lutheran tradition, and from a feminist perspective, to propose solutions to the complex questions of God-language, especially in liturgy.

_____. *Keeping it Metaphoric, Making it Inclusive.* American Essays in Liturgy. Collegeville, Minn.: The Liturgical Press, 1996. This small book from a well-known expert in liturgical language argues convincingly that liturgical language must remain both metaphoric and inclusive. She proposes that liturgical texts be designed with great care to keep both dimensions in view.

_____. "Liturgical Considerations of the Myth of the Crown." *Worship* 66 (1992) 482–497. In the context of a broader analysis of monarchy in the Bible, the author discusses options for the expression "kingdom of God," such as realm, dominion, or sovereign (pp. 494–496), and the practical ramifications of changing this language.

_____. *Worship: Searching for Language.* Washington, D.C.: Pastoral Press, 1988. A collection of 20 articles written from an ecumenical perspective dealing with the religious use of language, especially in liturgy.

Ramshaw-Schmidt, Gail. *Christ in Sacred Speech: The Meaning of Liturgical Language.* Philadelphia: Fortress, 1986. A broad overview of the entire question of liturgical language; explains many basic concepts in liturgy.

_____. "De Divinis Nominibus: The Gender of God." *Worship* 56 (1982) 117–131. A study of the language used for God in the Christian tradition. Emphasizes the notion of metaphor, the need for balance in employing female and male imagery for God, and the warning not to imply sexual identity when using the language of "person" for God.

_____. "Naming the Trinity: Orthodoxy and Inclusivity." *Worship* 60 (1986) 491–498. Argues for naming God in Trinitarian terms as "Abba, Servant, and Paraclete" in order to supplement but not replace traditional Trinitarian language.

Routley, Erik. "Sexist Language: A View From a Distance." *Worship* 53 (1979) 2–11. An early and practical article on the problem of exclusive language in liturgical hymns that argues for a moratorium on hymnal production until issues of language can be resolved.

Roy, Louis. "Inclusive Language Regarding God." *Worship* 65 (1991) 207–215. A balanced and practical view of the need to maintain traditional language for God as Father while utilizing biblical imagery for God as a motherly figure.

Talbert, Charles H. "The Church and Inclusive Language for God?" *PerRS* 19 (1992) 421–439. A well reasoned article by a scholar who is sensitive to issues of inclusivity but who wishes to point out some serious distortions in feminist biblical interpretation.

*Trau, Jane Mary. "Exclusively Male Imagery in Religious Language." *Worship* 66 (1992) 310–326. A balanced argument for the need to reexamine exclusively male imagery for God.

*Watkins, Keith. *Faithful and Fair: Transcending Sexist Language in Worship.* Nashville: Abingdon, 1981. A practical and judicious book from a Protestant perspective, where ministers are freer to design their own worship services.

Withers, Barbara A., ed. *Language and the Church: Articles and Designs for Workshops.* National Council of the Churches of Christ in the U.S.A., 1984. A "how to" booklet, based upon the experimental *Inclusive-Language Lectionary* of the 1980s. Contains useful discussion starters and workshop suggestions, but its Protestant orientation toward worship does not easily translate to a Roman Catholic liturgical setting.

Wren, Brian. *What Language Shall I Borrow? God-Talk in Worship: A Male Response to Feminist Theology.* New York: Crossroad, 1990. An attempt by a male theologian and composer of liturgical music to wrestle with the question of inclusive language. Many of his suggestions for hymnic language are controversial.

Index to Scripture Citations

Genesis	
1:2	47
1:26-27	60
1:27	32, 33
1:28	33
2	14
6:2	22
6:4	22
9:6	60
42:5	23

Exodus	
3:6	48
3:14	29, 48
4:22	35
19:4	47

Leviticus	
20:10	64

Numbers	
11:12	33

Deuteronomy	
22:22	64
32:6	35

32:11	47
32:11-12	47, 47n
32:18	14, 32, 33

2 Samuel	
7:14	35

1 Kings	22
10:1-10, 13	22

2 Kings	22
8:18	22
11:1-20	22
19:22	30

Tobit	
13:4	39

Job	
1:6	22

Psalms	
1:1	23, 23n, 60
2	84
2:7	31
3-7	23
8	61

8:3-4	61, 62	*Sirach*	
8:4	31	23:1	38
17:8	47	23:4	38
18:1-2	29	24:1-34	43
18:31	30	51:10	35, 38
18:46	30		
19:14	30	*Isaiah*	
22	23	1:4	30
26	23	5:19	30
28	23	5:24	30
28:1	30	10:17	30
29:1	22	31:5	47
36:7	47	42	32, 84
34:11	22	42:13	34
34:12	22	42:14	14, 32
51	23	45:10	34
57:1	47	46:3-4	14, 32, 34, 54
89:7	22	49:15	34
89:26	35	53	32, 84
91:1	47	62:5	45
91:4	47	63:16	35
103:13	34, 39	66:13	14, 32, 34
110	84		
110:1	31	*Jeremiah*	
		31:9	35
Proverbs			
1:20-33	43	*Baruch*	
2:16-19	43	3:9–4:4	43
3:13-18	43		
5:1-6	43	*Daniel*	
7:6-27	43	3:25	22
8:1-36	43	3:29	22
9:1-6	43	7	84
9:13-18	43	7:13	31, 62
Song of		*Hosea*	
Solomon	45	1:10	22
		2:1-20	45
Wisdom of Solomon		2:16	35, 45
2:16	38	2:19-20	45
7:22–9:18	43	3:1	35
11:10	38	11:1	35
14:3	38	11:9	30

Malachi

2:10	35, 39

Matthew

3:16	47
5:20	32
6:9	38
7:21	32
8:20	63
9:15	45
11:28-30	43
13:24	32
13:31-33	25
18:3	32
18:6	24
19:23-24	32
23:13	32
23:37	14, 32, 35
24:30	63
25:31	32
25:34	32
26:29	32
26:64	63
28:5-6	44
28:19	36

Mark

1:10	47
1:15	32
2:19-20	45
10:15	32
12:26	48
16:6	44

Luke

3:22	47
5:34-35	45
9:23	23
11:2	38
13:18-21	24
13:34	14, 32, 35
14:27	24
14:36	38
15:1-10	25

15:8-10	14, 32
24:16	44
24:31	44
24:42-43	44

John

1:1-8	43
1:14	43
1:29	43
1:32	47
1:36	43
3:29	45
6:35	43
6:35-65	23
8:1-11	63-64
8:3-6	64
8:12	43
8:24	29
8:28	29
8:58	29
11:25	43
13:19	29
14:6	43
14:15-16	46
14:26	46
15:1	43
15:1-27	23
15:5	23
15:26	46
16:7-11	46
19:36	43
20:14-16	44
21:7	44
21:12	44

Acts of the Apostles 70

1:11	44
7:1	22
9	44
9:4-5	44
22:7-8	44
26:14-15	44

Romans

8:14	22–23
8:15	38, 39
13:14	42

1 Corinthians 73

1:24	43
10:16-17	16
11:2-16	25
12:4-6	36
12:13	74
14:34-35	25
14:34-36	25
15:9-10	44

2 Corinthians

11:2	45
11:5	44
13:13	36

Galatians

3:26-28	74
3:27	42
4:6	38, 39

Ephesians

3:14-16	39
4:22-24	42
5:21-24	25
5:21-33	25
5:22-32	45
5:23	25n

Colossians

3:9-10	42
3:11	74
3:18	25
3:18-21	25

2 Thessalonians

2:13-14	36

1 Timothy 22

2 Timothy 22

Titus 22

Philemon

20	22

Hebrews

2:5-18	80
2:6	62
2:9	31
4:12	27

1 Peter

1:2	36
2:4-5	80
2:9	80

Revelation

5:6	43
12	45, 85
14:1	43
14:14	63
21:23	43

Old Testament Apocrypha

3 Maccabees

2:21	38–39
5:7	38
6:3	38
6:8	38
7:6	38–39

Qumran Literature

4Q372	38